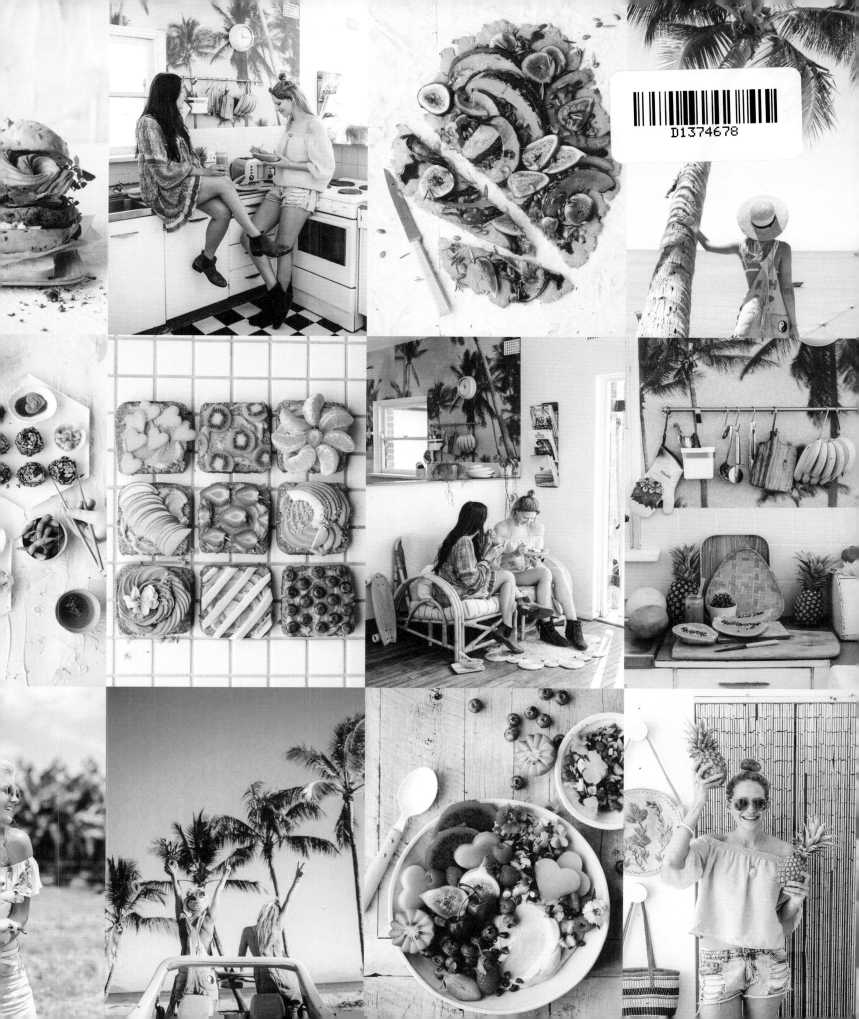

Cowboy Caviar (serves 8 261 cals)

2 cans black-eyed peas
1 can black beans
1 can corn
3/4 pound tomatoes
1 red, orange or yellow pepper
1/2 small red onion, chopped
1/2 cup coriander leaves & stems.
1-2 chillies, ribs removed, seeded, finely chopped
1 avocado (optional) (add last)

mix in a bowl

Italian dressing

1/3 cup olive oil
3 tbsp red wine vinegar or lime juice
2 cloves garlic, minced
1-1/2 tsp salt
1 tsp dried oregano
1/2 tsp dried basil
1 tsp honey
1/8 tsp chilli flakes
Black pepper to taste

whisk & drizzle over beans. Leave to marinate for at least 20 minutes.

Vegan Kitchen

PUBLISHED IN 2017 BY OCTOPUS PUBLISHING GROUP LIMITED
BASED ON MATERIALS LICENSED TO IT BY BAUER MEDIA BOOKS, AUSTRALIA

BAUER MEDIA BOOKS IS A DIVISION OF
BAUER MEDIA PTY LIMITED,
54 PARK ST, SYDNEY; GPO BOX 4088,
SYDNEY, NSW 2001, AUSTRALIA
PH +61 2 9282 8618; FAX +61 2 9126 3702
WWW.AWWCOOKBOOKS.COM.AU

Bauer Media Books

PUBLISHER
JO RUNCIMAN

EDITORIAL & FOOD DIRECTOR
PAMELA CLARK

DIRECTOR OF SALES, MARKETING & RIGHTS
BRIAN CEARNES

CREATIVE DIRECTOR & DESIGNER
HANNAH BLACKMORE

FOOD CONCEPT DIRECTOR & FOOD EDITOR
SOPHIA YOUNG

SENIOR EDITOR
STEPHANIE KISTNER

JUNIOR EDITOR
AMANDA LEES

OPERATIONS MANAGER
DAVID SCOTTO

PRINTED IN CHINA
BY LEO PAPER PRODUCTS LTD

PUBLISHED AND DISTRIBUTED IN THE UNITED KINGDOM
BY OCTOPUS PUBLISHING GROUP LTD
CARMELITE HOUSE
50 VICTORIA EMBANKMENT
LONDON, EC4Y 0DZ
UNITED KINGDOM
INFO@OCTOPUS-PUBLISHING.CO.UK;
WWW.OCTOPUSBOOKS.CO.UK

INTERNATIONAL FOREIGN LANGUAGE RIGHTS
BRIAN CEARNES, BAUER MEDIA BOOKS
BCEARNES@BAUER-MEDIA.COM.AU

A CATALOGUE RECORD FOR THIS BOOK IS AVAILABLE
FROM THE NATIONAL LIBRARY OF AUSTRALIA.
ISBN 9781742458519 (HARDBACK)

THE AUSTRALIAN
Women's Weekly

Vegan Kitchen

Contents

Plant Food Love

WHETHER YOU ARE ALREADY VEGAN OR SIMPLY VEGAN-CURIOUS, INTEREST IN EXPLORING THE INCREDIBLE RANGE OF PLANT-BASED FOODS HAS NEVER BEEN AS POPULAR AS IT IS NOW.

WHAT IS A VEGAN DIET?

A vegan diet is entirely plant-based, excluding all animal products. Not only are meat, seafood, eggs and dairy products off the menu, but also honey and gelatine. Whether it's for animal welfare, ecological or health reasons, veganism is becoming a more mainstream choice. After all, if you are already vegetarian or have family members or friends who are, and you enjoy sharing meals together, it's not a huge leap to eliminate all animal-based food from your diet.

THE VEGAN KITCHEN

Veganism has often been characterised as restrictive, difficult and just plain hard work. Instead of focusing on what vegans don't eat, let's look at the abundance of ingredients vegans can enjoy. In addition to the huge – and growing – range of vegetables and fruits on offer at greengrocers, farmers' markets and supermarkets, a vegan kitchen generally includes:

Legumes Includes dried and canned lentils, chickpeas, cannellini beans, kidney beans, borlotti beans, black-eye beans and green and yellow split peas (see page 9 for more information).

Grains and grain substitutes/pseudo-grains Includes amaranth, barley, buckwheat, freekeh, oats, rice, faro, millet, polenta, quinoa, and wheat-based products such as flours, couscous and burghul (see page 9 for more information).

Nuts and seeds Almonds, cashews, peanuts, pecans, pistachios, macadamias, walnuts, sunflower seeds, pepitas, linseeds, chia seeds

and sesame seeds, as well as unhulled and hulled tahini (see page 9 for more information).

Soy products Such as tofu, tempeh and other soy products, including miso and 'cheeses' (see page 9 for more information).

Alternative milks There is a wide range of milks now available, including soy milk, rice milk, almond milk, coconut milk and oat milk.

Sea vegetables Includes nori, kombu, wakame and spirulina (see page 9 for more information).

Herbs and spices Keep a ready supply of spices such as cardamom, cinnamon, cloves, coriander, cumin, fennel seeds, garam masala, garlic powder, ginger, mustard seeds and powder, nutmeg, onion powder, paprika and turmeric. Fresh herbs, such as basil, coriander, dill, flat-leaf parsley, mint, oregano, rosemary, and thyme add flavour and freshness.

Condiments Including soy sauce, tamari, miso, vinegars, mustards and nutritional yeast flakes (see page 9 for more information).

Sweeteners Try using pure maple syrup, coconut sugar, agave syrup and rice malt syrup instead of regular cane sugar.

GETTING STARTED

For anyone considering making the transition to a plant-based diet, it's a good idea to start slowly. Maybe try introducing one or two vegan meals each week, then progressing onto a couple of vegan days. Gradual changes are more likely to be sustainable. When thinking about changing your eating habits, it's important to make sensible decisions and consider how to balance what you eat to include a variety of foods that provide essential nutrients, such as iron, protein, vitamins, minerals, Omega-3 fatty acids, fibre and carbohydrates. By planning well and following a sensible approach, it is possible to meet your dietary needs with a vegan diet. Consult a nutritionist, dietitian or medical practitioner, if in any doubt.

YOUR NUTRITIONAL NEEDS

When planning vegan meals, especially when starting out, the most frequently asked questions are about how to incorporate all the necessary nutrients into your diet. To help avoid potential deficiencies, here are the most common nutrients that cause concern and suggestions for vegan sources to meet your dietary needs:

Calcium In place of dairy products, use nuts, seeds, leafy green vegetables, legumes, and soy products, especially those that are fortified with calcium.

Iodine Include sea vegetables, such as nori, kombu or wakame and small amounts of iodised salt. Check with your doctor before taking supplements if you have a thyroid issue.

Iron Eat nuts, lentils, oats, dried fruit, dark leafy green vegetables and soy products. Eating these in tandem with a vitamin C-rich food aids the body to absorb the iron.

Omega-3 fatty acids Include linseeds, chia seeds, pepitas, seaweed, spirulina and walnuts.

Protein Eat legumes, whole grains, quinoa, nuts, seeds and soy products, especially tofu and tempeh.

Vitamin B12 As this is only found in meat, incorporate foods fortified with vitamin B-12, such as some cereals, plant-based milks and soy products. A supplement can be taken for healthy blood cells.

Vitamin C Include tomatoes, red capsicum, broccoli, citrus fruit and berries in your diet.

Zinc Add whole grains, nuts, pepitas, wheatgerm and soy products, especially tofu and tempeh to your diet.

Vegan pantry

PROBIOTICS are micro-organisms found in lactic acid bacteria, yeast and moulds. They work in tandem with prebiotics, non-digestible food fibres to support good gut health. Vegan sources include: sauerkraut (1), kimchi, kefir, miso, tempeh and kombucha. Prebiotic-rich foods include: oats, legumes, green vegetables and bananas.

LEGUMES are an essential in the vegan diet, providing high protein, slow-release carbs and are a useful source of the B-group vitamins, especially folate. They also contain iron, magnesium, calcium and zinc. From tiny quick-cooking lentils to larger beans, like chickpeas (2), and even peanuts, which are technically a legume, all are valuable.

NUTRITIONAL POWDERS are great flavour boosters with powerful antioxidants. Matcha powder (3), dried green tea, works in both sweet and savoury dishes (see our Matcha Mint Slice, page 236). Acai powder, from an Amazon wild berry is another to try in smoothies or raw puddings. Raw cacao, wtih a bitter taste retains more of its nutrients than cocoa.

CHIA SEEDS (4) are a particularly rich source of omega-3 fatty acids, which is more commonly found in fish and meat, and soluble fibre. As with all seeds they are nutritionally dense, providing protein, a variety of vitamins, minerals and trace elements. And like sesame seeds, chia seeds are high in calcium. Also add pepitas, linseeds and sunflower seeds to your pantry.

SOY PRODUCTS such as tempeh (5), tofu and soy all provide vegans with a high-quality source of protein, complete with essential amino acids. They are also low in unsaturated fats (the exception is tofu puffs) and contain B vitamins. However, there is a question mark around high consumption of soy products and its potential to harm male fertility.

NUTRITIONAL YEAST FLAKES (6) are a seasoning used to provide a moreish cheese-like umami taste (see our Moxarella recipe, page 158). To get the most bang for your buck, buy a brand that is fortified with B12, a vitamin required for the development of healthy blood cells and the prevention of anaemia, which is only available from fortified foods or via a supplement on a vegan diet.

NUTS add a wide spectrum of nutrients to a vegan diet. They provide a combination of healthy monounsaturated and polyunsaturated fats, moderate amounts of protein and dietary fibre. Some can be singled out for unique attributes: almonds (7) for protein, calcium and magnesium; cashews for iron and walnuts for plant omega-3 fatty acids.

GRAINS that are whole and unrefined have the most nutritional benefits and help with satiety. The cooking properties of quinoa (8) mean that although it is a seed it is referred to as a pseudo-grain. It is one of a few plant-based foods that contain all essential amino acids, making it a complete protein. And also because it's not technically a grain, it's completely gluten-free.

SEA VEGETABLES such as nori (9), wakami, kelp and kombu are rich with nutrients and are a source of essential vitamins and minerals. In particular they are high in iodine, needed for healthy thyroid function, which in turn aids metabolism. Too much iodine can be just as damaging as too little, so as with most foods, eat broadly and avoid supplements without consulting your doctor.

Breakfast

Nut & seed butter

THIS DELICIOUS NON-DAIRY BUTTER ALTERNATIVE IS SUITABLE NOT ONLY FOR VEGANS BUT ALSO FOR THOSE WHO ARE LACTOSE INTOLERANT.

This butter is very lightly sweetened, but can still be used as a spread for savoury sandwiches. Simply omit the maple syrup if you prefer.

- **1 cup (160g) blanched almonds, roasted**
- **½ cup (70g) roasted unsalted peanuts**
- **½ cup (75g) sunflower seed kernels**
- **¼ cup (40g) linseeds (flaxseeds)**
- **¼ cup (60ml) olive oil**
- **1 tablespoon pure maple syrup**
- **½ teaspoon sea salt flakes**

1 Process all ingredients, scraping the side of the bowl regularly, until the mixture is smooth. Alternatively, use a high-powered blender for a faster and smoother result. (This step may take up to 25 minutes depending on the processing power of your processor or blender. Powerful commercial processors and blenders will take around 10 minutes, while small retail home-use blenders/processors can take up to 25 minutes before the mixture becomes smooth.)

2 Spoon nut and seed butter into a jar and refrigerate. Stir the nut butter before using as the oil will settle on the top.

TIP Nut and seed butter will keep refrigerated in an airtight container for up to 3 weeks.

VARIATION For a 'Nutella-like' spread, add 1½ tablespoons dutch-processed cocoa and an extra 1 tablespoon maple syrup to the ingredients.

OTHER IDEAS For crunchy nut butter, reserve ½ cup of the nuts and pulse through at the end of blending.

SWAP The almonds and peanuts with cashews and macadamias; omit the linseeds, and stir in 2 tablespoons poppy seeds at the end.

SERVING IDEAS Spread the nut butter on your favourite toast or crispbread, then top with fruit, such as sliced rockmelon, kiwifruit, mandarin segments, thinly sliced apple, sliced strawberries, sliced avocado with sesame seeds or edible flowers, sliced banana or blueberries.

Coconut yoghurt

THIS COCONUT MILK YOGHURT IS NOT SUITABLE FOR COOKING. IT IS BEST ENJOYED FOR BREAKFAST OR AS DESSERT TOPPED WITH FRESH OR POACHED FRUIT.

You will need to start this recipe 3 days ahead to allow time for fermentation. The yoghurt mixture is poured into sterilised jars to set; before you start this recipe, see glossary, page 283 for information on sterilising jars.

- **¼ cup (30g) tapioca flour**
- **800ml canned coconut milk (see tips)**
- **400ml canned coconut cream (see tips)**
- **3 probiotic capsules (see tips)**
- **1 tablespoon pure maple syrup**
- **fresh fruit and edible flowers, to serve (see serving ideas)**

1 Sterilise jars (see glossary, page 283).

2 Whisk tapioca flour and ¼ cup of the coconut milk in a small bowl until smooth and combined.

3 Pour tapioca mixture into a medium saucepan; whisk in remaining coconut milk and the coconut cream until combined. Stir mixture over low heat for 10 minutes or until it boils and thickens. Remove pan from heat; place a cooking thermometer in the pan, then stand until mixture cools to 43°C/109°F. Once cooled, open probiotic capsules; add the powder and maple syrup and stir to combine.

4 Transfer mixture to warm sterilised jars; seal immediately. Stand in a warm place for 12 hours or until cultured (the mixture will taste slightly sour) and thickened slightly. Refrigerate for 24 hours or until coconut yoghurt thickens further. Coconut yoghurt will keep refrigerated for up to 2 weeks.

TIPS Tapioca flour is gluten-free and available from major supermarkets, health-food stores and Asian grocers. Buy coconut milk and coconut cream without additives, preservatives and stabilisers, otherwise the set of the yoghurt might be affected.
Probiotic capsules are available from pharmacies and health-food stores.
SERVING IDEAS Serve topped with kiwifruit, figs, blueberries, raspberries and edible flowers. You can use any combination of seasonal fruits you prefer.

Cherry tomato &
'cream cheese' bruschetta

IF YOU HAVE IT, DAY OLD-BREAD IS IDEAL FOR BRUSCHETTA. IT WILL BE REVIVED BY THE GORGEOUS TOMATO JUICES AND STILL RETAIN ITS TEXTURE.

- 400g (12½ ounces) truss tomato medley mix
- 250g (8 ounces) truss cherry tomatoes
- 1 tablespoon fresh rosemary leaves
- 4 cloves garlic, bruised, halved
- 2 tablespoons olive oil
- 2 tablespoons sticky fig and balsamic vinegar drizzle
- 8 thick slices (600g) soy and linseed sourdough bread
- ⅔ cup (150g) tofu 'cream cheese' (see tips) or moxarella (see page 158)
- rocket and walnut pesto (see page 43), optional

1 Preheat oven to 180°C/350°F.
2 Place tomatoes, rosemary and garlic on a medium oven tray. Drizzle with oil and vinegar; season well. Roast for 20 minutes. Cool for 5 minutes. Crush tomatoes lightly; reserve juices on tray.
3 Meanwhile, toast sourdough slices.
4 Spread 'cream cheese' on toast; top with tomato mixture. Drizzle with juices from tray and pesto.

TIPS Use balsamic vinegar if you cannot find fig balsamic vinegar.
Made from soy beans, non-hydrogenated canola oil, vegetable gums, lactic acid and potassium sorbate, this tofu-based 'cream cheese' is available in the refrigerator section of supermarkets.
SWAP You can use oregano instead of rosemary. For a soy-free version, use mashed avocado instead of the 'cream cheese' and rye bread instead of the soy and linseed.
SERVING IDEA For lunch or a light dinner, serve with a side salad topped with sunflower seeds.

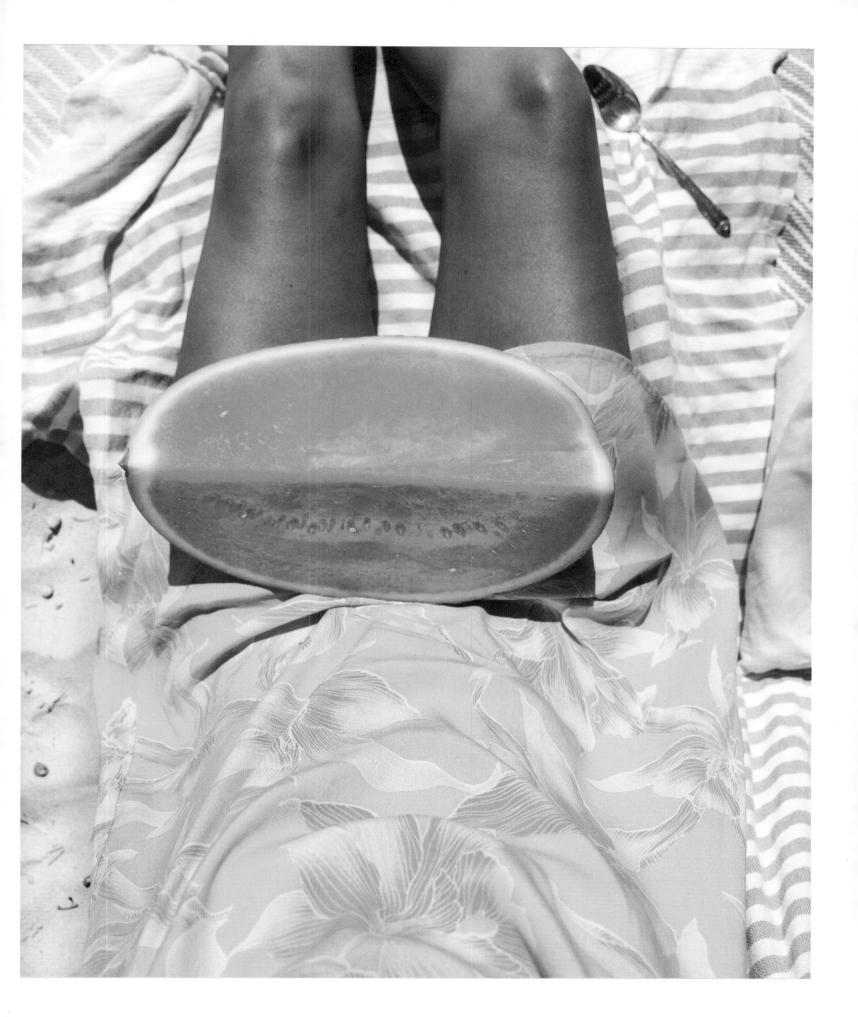

Protein warrior smoothie

EATING PROTEIN IN THE MORNING HAS BEEN SHOWN TO REDUCE THE AMOUNT OF CALORIES CONSUMED LATER IN THE DAY AS A RESULT OF ITS SATIATING EFFECT.

- **1½ cups (250g) frozen chopped mango**
- **2 small bananas (260g)**
- **½ teaspoon ground cinnamon**
- **1 tablespoon chia seeds**
- **2 teaspoons linseeds (flaxseeds)**
- **1 tablespoon almond spread**
- **2 tablespoons pea protein powder**
- **1 tablespoon coconut syrup**
- **1¾ cups (430ml) coconut water (see tips)**
- **1 cup ice**
- **2 teaspoons unsweetened flaked coconut, optional**
- **baby mint leaves and edible flowers, optional**

1 Blend all ingredients, except flaked coconut, mint and edible flowers, until smooth.

2 Pour smoothie into two large milkshake glasses. Top with flaked coconut, mint and edible flowers.

TIPS You can use the water from a fresh young coconut for the coconut water, or purchase coconut water from the supermarket or health food store. If using a fresh young coconut, you may need to add water to make up the required amount. Keep linseeds in the fridge or freezer, as they can become rancid in the cupboard. Brown rice protein can be used in place of pea protein powder.

This smoothie is a great breakfast or post-workout snack; it makes 1 litre (4 cups).

Crunch bowl with berry coconut yoghurt

SEEDS ARE A GOOD SOURCE OF PROTEIN, FIBRE AND MINERALS. PEPITAS CONTAIN A SURPRISING AMOUNT OF IRON FOR THEIR SIZE.

- **1 cup (160g) brazil nuts**
- **½ cup (80g) almond kernels**
- **⅓ cup (50g) pepitas (pumpkin seed kernels)**
- **⅓ cup (50g) sunflower seed kernels**
- **⅔ cup (30g) unsweetened flaked coconut**
- **¼ cup (35g) cacao nibs**
- **⅔ cup (110g) inca berries**
- **3 cups (420g) berry coconut yoghurt**
- **fresh fruit and edible flowers, to serve (see serving ideas)**

1 Preheat oven to 180°C/350°F.
2 Place brazil nuts and almonds on an oven tray; roast for 10 minutes or until browned lightly and fragrant. Chop nuts coarsely; place in a large bowl. Roast seeds on oven tray for 8 minutes or until browned lightly; add to bowl. Roast coconut on oven tray for 4 minutes or until browned lightly and fragrant. Add to bowl with cacao nibs and inca berries; stir to combine.
3 Spoon crunch bowl mixture into serving bowls, then the yoghurt. Serve topped fruit and edible flowers.

TIPS Any combination of nuts and seeds can be used in this recipe. Inca berries are also known as cape gooseberries and have a wonderful tangy flavour. They are high in vitamins C, B and A and are available at some supermarkets and health food stores.
OTHER IDEAS Serve the crunch bowl mix as a muesli, or sprinkle on top of yoghurt or fruit, scattered with edible flowers and vegan chocolate, if you like. It also doubles as a trail mix for an energy-rich snack on the go.
SERVING IDEAS Serve crunch bowl topped with dragonfruit, honeydew, figs, kiwifruit, cherries, blueberries, strawberries, pomegranate seeds and raspberries. You can use any combination of seasonal fruits you prefer.

Nutty beetroot & berry cobb

A WARM PLACE FOR PROVING CAN BE ON THE OPEN OVEN DOOR WITH THE HEAT ON LOW, A SUNNY DRAUGHT-FREE SPOT OR NEAR A HEATER.

- ½ cup (125ml) almond milk
- ½ cup (125ml) lukewarm filtered water
- ¼ cup (60ml) olive oil
- 2 tablespoons pure maple syrup
- 1½ teaspoons instant dry yeast
- 2 cups (260g) wholemeal spelt flour
- 2 cups (260g) white spelt flour
- 3 teaspoons sea salt flakes
- 2 teaspoons ground allspice
- 1 cup (125g) coarsely grated beetroot (beets)
- ⅔ cup (70g) chopped walnuts
- ½ cup (70g) dried inca berries
- 1 tablespoon olive oil, extra
- 1 tablespoon white spelt flour, extra

1 Combine almond milk, the water, oil, maple syrup and yeast in a large jug. Stand in a warm place for 5 minutes or until mixture is frothy.

2 Meanwhile, place flours, salt, allspice, beetroot, walnuts and inca berries in the bowl of a stand mixer with a dough hook. Mix for 10 seconds to combine. With mixer operating on medium speed, gradually add the yeast mixture. Beat for 4 minutes or until dough is smooth and elastic.

3 Knead dough on bench until smooth. Coat dough in extra oil then return to bowl; cover with plastic wrap. Stand in a warm place for 1 hour or until doubled in size. Punch the dough down then form into a round. Sprinkle a sheet of baking paper with half the extra flour; place dough on top. Cover with plastic wrap; stand in a warm place to prove for 30 minutes.

4 Meanwhile, preheat oven to 180°C/350°F; place a pizza stone in the centre of the oven while heating.

5 Using a sharp knife, make four cuts on top of the dough, into a square shape without connecting the corners; sprinkle with remaining extra flour. Slide dough off paper onto pizza stone.

6 Bake for 30 minutes. Increase oven temperature to 220°C/425°F; bake for a further 10 minutes or until bread sounds hollow when you tap the base. Cool on a wire rack.

DO-AHEAD Bread is best made on day of serving but can be toasted after that. Slice, then freeze for up to 2 months.
SERVING IDEAS Serve toasted bread spread with tofu 'cream cheese' with matcha and a drizzle of maple syrup.

Buckini & berry muesli clusters

SERVE CLUSTERS WITH NUT, OAT OR SOY MILK AND VEGAN COCONUT YOGHURT, OR SPRINKLE OVER STONE FRUIT OR BERRIES AS A CRUNCHY TOPPING.

- **1 cup (110g) rolled oats**
- **1 teaspoon ground allspice**
- **½ teaspoon ground cardamom**
- **½ teaspoon sea salt flakes**
- **2 tablespoons rice malt syrup**
- **1 tablespoon coconut oil, melted**
- **1 cup (180g) activated buckinis (see tips)**
- **1 cup (30g) puffed quinoa**
- **1 cup (30g) puffed buckwheat**
- **¼ cup (30g) goji berries**
- **¼ cup (35g) dried cranberries**
- **¼ cup (40g) chia seeds**
- **¾ cup (75g) freeze-dried pomegranate seeds**

1 Preheat oven to 180°C/350°F.

2 Place oats on a large shallow-sided oven tray. Sprinkle with spices and salt then drizzle with syrup and oil; toss to coat. Bake for 10 minutes or until mixture is sticky and golden, stirring once during cooking. Cool, then break into clusters. Use a spatula to scrape the mixture from the tray as it will be caramelised.

3 Place remaining ingredients in a large bowl with oat clusters; toss to combine. Place in a glass jar or airtight container.

TIPS Activated buckinis are soaked and dehydrated buckwheat, which are gluten-free and high in protein, available in some health food stores. You can replace puffed quinoa or buckwheat with puffed rice. Any dried fruit would work well. Try to buy sulphate-free dried fruit that has no added sugar. Freeze-dried pomegranate seeds are available from some supermarkets and health food stores. To make your own muesli bars, heat some rice malt syrup until bubbling and beginning to caramelise; toss through muesli, then press into a lined slice pan. Cool, then cut into bars.

DO-AHEAD Muesli keeps in an airtight container at room temperature for up to 2 months.

PREP TIME 10 MINUTES (+ STANDING)
MAKES 2 CUPS

Nut milks

YOU CAN MAKE NUT MILKS WITH MOST NUTS: HAZELNUTS, ALMONDS, CASHEWS, PECANS. IF YOU WANT TO SWEETEN THE MILK, ADD PURE MAPLE SYRUP OR PUREED DATES.

Place 1 cup (140g) skinless hazelnuts in a large bowl; cover with cold water. Stand, covered, for 4 hours or overnight. Drain; rinse under cold water. Drain. Process nuts with 2 cups (500ml) water until smooth. Pour mixture through a strainer lined with a fine cloth into a large bowl. Keep any blended nuts left behind for another use.

TIPS Using skinless or blanched nuts will create a whiter coloured milk. Dry out the strained, blended nuts on an oven tray in a 150°C/300°F oven. Sprinkle on your breakfast cereal or add to curries and pastes.
Using a high-powered blender, such as a Vitamix, will create a smoother textured milk.

spiced nut milk Make nut milk above using 1 cup pecans. Stir in 2 cinnamon sticks, 3 star anise and either ¼ teaspoon saffron threads or 2 long strips orange rind; leave overnight for flavours to infuse.

vanilla nut milk Make nut milk above using ½ cup almonds and ½ cup cashews. Split a vanilla bean lengthways, scrape the seeds into the milk; stir to combine.

Scrambled tofu wraps

TO DIAL-UP THE FLAVOUR EVEN FURTHER ON THIS WRAP, DRIZZLE IT WITH THE GREEN GODDESS TAHINI YOGHURT (PAGE 80) AND EXTRA HOT CHILLI SAUCE.

- 600g (1¼ pounds) firm tofu
- 1 tablespoon olive oil
- 1 tablespoon tamari
- 30g (1 ounce) baby spinach, sliced thinly
- 1 large tomato (220g), chopped
- 2 green onions (scallions), chopped finely
- 1 cup (240g) canned refried beans with chilli
- 4 x 21cm (8½-inch) red quinoa wraps or tortillas (100g)
- 1 medium avocado (250g), chopped
- ⅓ cup loosely packed fresh coriander (cilantro) leaves
- hot chilli sauce, to taste
- 1 lime (65g), cut into wedges

1 Pat tofu dry with paper towel. Crumble tofu into pieces with your fingers.

2 Heat the oil in a large frying pan over medium heat; cook tofu and tamari, stirring, for 2 minutes or until warmed through. Add spinach, tomato and green onion and cook for 1 minute. Season to taste. Remove from pan; cover to keep warm.

3 Stir beans in a small saucepan over low heat until hot. Spread beans on wraps; top with tofu mixture, avocado, coriander and sauce. Roll up to enclose; tie with kitchen string, if you like. Serve with lime wedges.

TIPS For a milder flavour, you can use plain refried beans and omit the hot chilli sauce. The beans can be heated in the microwave.
DO-AHEAD The recipe is best made close to serving.

Spiced banana bread

FOR A REALLY GOOD BANANA TASTE YOU WILL NEED 2 MASHED LARGE OVERRIPE BANANAS (460G) FOR BREAD, PLUS 2 SMALLER JUST-RIPE BANANAS TO TOP THE LOAF.

- 1¼ cups (185g) self-raising flour
- 1 cup (130g) spelt flour
- 1 teaspoon baking powder
- 2 teaspoons ground cinnamon
- 1 teaspoon ground cardamom
- 1 teaspoon ground ginger
- 1 teaspoon vanilla powder
- 1 tablespoon white chia seeds
- ¾ cup (75g) walnuts, chopped coarsely
- 1 cup (240g) mashed overripe bananas
- ¾ cup (180ml) almond milk
- ⅓ cup (70g) coconut oil, melted
- 2 small bananas (260g), extra, halved lengthways
- 2 tablespoons pure maple syrup
- ⅓ cup (90g) cashew cream (see tips)
- pure maple syrup, extra
- edible flowers, optional

1 Preheat oven to 180°C/350°F. Grease and line a 9cm x 19cm (3¾-inch x 7¾-inch) loaf pan.

2 Sift flours, baking powder, spices and vanilla powder into a large bowl; stir in seeds and ½ cup of the walnuts. Make a well in the centre. Add combined mashed banana, almond milk and coconut oil to dry ingredients; stir until just combined.

3 Spread mixture into pan. Top with remaining walnuts and extra banana. Bake for 50 minutes or until a skewer inserted into the centre comes out clean. Brush loaf with maple syrup. Cool in pan for 15 minutes; turn out onto a wire rack.

4 Serve slices of loaf warm or cooled with cashew cream, drizzled with a little extra maple syrup and edible flowers, if you like.

TIPS Loaves tend to crack because of the small surface area. To test if a loaf is cooked, insert the skewer as close to the centre as possible, but not through a crack; a crack will give an inaccurate result. Cashew cream is available from health food stores or serve with vegan yoghurt (see page 40).

Chia crêpes with caramelised banana & black sesame

THE HOTTER THE PAN THE BETTER THE CRÊPES, HOWEVER REMOVE THE PAN FROM THE HEAT FOR A FEW SECONDS BETWEEN EACH CRÊPE SO THAT THEY DON'T BURN.

- ¾ cup (110g) plain (all-purpose) flour
- 1 tablespoon white chia seeds
- 2½ tablespoons coconut sugar
- ½ teaspoon ground cinnamon
- 1 cup (250ml) almond milk
- ½ cup (125ml) water, approximately
- 30g (1 ounce) coconut oil, melted
- 4 sugar bananas (520g), halved lengthways (see tip)
- ⅔ cup (190g) coconut or vegan yoghurt
- 2 tablespoons blueberries
- 2 teaspoons black sesame seeds

1 Combine flour, chia seeds, 2 teaspoons of the coconut sugar and the cinnamon in a medium bowl. Make a well in the centre; gradually whisk in combine almond milk and water, until smooth. Stand for 20 minutes.

2 Heat a 26cm (10½-inch) (top measurement) non-stick frying pan over a high heat. Lightly grease with some of the coconut oil. Pour ½ cup of the batter into the centre of the hot pan, tilting pan to coat the base in a thin layer; cook for 1 minute or until browned. Turn, cook on the other side until golden. Transfer to a plate; cover with foil to keep warm. Repeat with remaining batter, greasing with coconut oil, to make a total of 4 crêpes.

3 Reduce heat under pan to medium-high heat. Sprinkle remaining sugar on cut-side of the banana halves. Cook cut-side down in pan for 1 minute or until caramelised.

4 Divide crêpes between plates. Top with caramelised banana, yoghurt and blueberries; sprinkle with sesame seeds.

TIP Sugar bananas, also known as finger bananas are smaller and sweeter than regular bananas. If unavailable halve regular bananas lengthways and crossways.

Spiced pecan french toast

THE TRICK TO COOKING THIS TOAST PERFECTLY IS TO KEEP AN EYE ON THE HEAT SO THAT THE NUTS DON'T SCORCH.

- 1½ cups (375ml) coconut milk
- 2 teaspoons vanilla extract
- ½ cup (125ml) pure maple syrup
- ⅓ cup (35g) hazelnut meal
- 1 tablespoon nutritional yeast flakes (see tips)
- ½ teaspoon mixed spice
- 1 cup (120g) pecans, chopped finely
- 8 x 50g (1½-ounce) slices thick multigrain sourdough bread
- 40g (1½ ounces) vegan margarine spread
- 250g (8 ounces) mixed berries
- 2 teaspoons icing (confectioners') sugar
- edible flowers, optional

1 Whisk coconut milk, vanilla, 2 tablespoons of the syrup, the hazelnut meal, yeast and mixed spice in a shallow dish. Place pecans on a plate. Soak bread in coconut milk mixture, one at a time, for 1 minute each side. Press onto pecans.

2 Heat half the margarine in a large frying pan over low-medium heat; cook bread, in batches, for 2 minutes each side or until golden, adding remaining margarine halfway through cooking.

3 Divide french toast among plates; top with berries and remaining syrup. Dust with icing sugar; served topped with edible flowers.

TIPS Nutritional yeast is deactivated yeast that is a complete protein, as it contains 18 amino acids, including the nine that are essential for good health. It is generally fortified with B12, an important nutrient for vegans that is lacking in a meat-free diet. It is available from health food stores. SWAP Almond meal for hazelnut meal and olive oil for vegan magarine spread.

Vegan yoghurt

THIS IS NOT A TRUE YOGHURT
AS IT IS NOT CULTURED. IT'S
MORE OF A NUT CREAM TO BE
USED AS AN EASY STAND IN FOR
THOSE TIMES WHEN YOU NEED
A VEGAN REPLACEMENT FOR
DAIRY YOGHURT. FOR CULTURED
COCONUT YOGHURT, SEE PAGE 15.

Place 1 cup (150g) cashews and 1 cup (160g) whole
blanched almonds in a large bowl; cover with cold water.
Stand, covered, for 4 hours or overnight. Drain nuts;
rinse under cold water, drain well. Blend nuts in a high-
powered blender with 1 cup (250ml) water until it forms
a yoghurt-like consistency. Store in an airtight container
in the fridge for up to 1 week.

TIPS You can experiment with different nuts to create this
yoghurt, bearing in mind the flavour of each nut.
TRY Stir in the juice of 1 lemon for a great savoury yoghurt
option to add to salads or top soups and curries.
SERVING IDEAS Top with edible flowers for a summery feel.

passionfruit yoghurt Make vegan yoghurt above,
then stir in the pulp of 3 passionfruit.

strawberry yoghurt Make vegan yoghurt above, using
1 cup (150g) cashews and 1 cup (120g) pecans. Blend
or process 250g (8 ounces) strawberries until smooth.
Fold strawberry puree through yoghurt to create a
swirled effect, then top with extra strawberries.

Brekkie mushroom burger

PORTOBELLOS HAVE A MOREISH SAVOURY TASTE KNOWN AS 'UMAMI', ARE A GOOD SOURCE OF B VITAMINS AND ARE ALSO THE ONLY VEGAN SOURCES OF VITAMIN D.

- **8 x 100g (3-ounce) large portobello mushrooms, trimmed**
- **½ cup (125ml) olive oil**
- **1 medium eggplant (300g), cut into 4 slices crossways**
- **400g (12½ ounces) tomatoes, sliced thickly**
- **1 tablespoon balsamic vinegar**
- **2 small avocados (400g), sliced thinly**
- **100g (3 ounces) baby spinach**

ROCKET & WALNUT PESTO
- **50g (1½ ounces) baby rocket (arugula) leaves**
- **½ cup firmly packed fresh basil leaves**
- **½ cup (50g) walnuts**
- **1 clove garlic, crushed**
- **1½ tablespoons nutritional yeast flakes (see Vegan Pantry, page 9)**
- **½ cup (125ml) olive oil**
- **2 tablespoons lemon juice**

1 Preheat oven to 200°C/400°F. Line three oven trays with baking paper.
2 Place mushrooms cup-side up, on two trays. Drizzle with 2 tablespoons of the oil; season. Place eggplant on remaining tray. Drizzle with ¼ cup of the remaining oil. Roast vegetables for 20 minutes. Toss tomatoes in remaining oil and the vinegar in a medium bowl; place on tray around mushrooms. Roast vegetables for a further 15 minutes or until tender.
3 Meanwhile, make rocket and walnut pesto.
4 Place four mushrooms, cup-side up, on plates. Top with eggplant, tomato, avocado, spinach, pesto and remaining mushrooms, cup-side down. Season.

rocket & walnut pesto Blend or process rocket, basil, walnuts, garlic and yeast flakes until combined. Add oil in a thin steady stream, blending until smooth. Add juice; blend until just combined. If pesto is too thick, add 1 tablespoon water. Season to taste. (Makes 1 cup)

TIP Store any leftover pesto covered by a thin film of olive oil in the fridge for up to 1 week. Use in sandwiches or swirled through vegetable soups.
DO-AHEAD Pesto can be made a day ahead; keep tightly covered in the fridge. It can also be frozen in a small container for up to 3 months.

food just tastes better
when you share it with
your best friends

Fig & orange chia puddings

FIGS AND CHIA SEEDS ARE SOURCES OF DIETARY FIBRE AND PROTEIN, WHICH PROVIDE SATIETY. THEY, ALONG WITH ALMONDS, ARE ALL NON-DAIRY SOURCES OF CALCIUM.

- 5 dried turkish figs (80g)
- 1 cup (250ml) water
- 2 cups (500ml) almond milk
- ½ teaspoon vanilla bean powder
- 1 tablespoon pure maple syrup
- 1 teaspoon finely grated orange rind
- ½ cup (80g) white chia seeds
- 1 cup (280g) coconut yoghurt
- 150g (4½ ounces) blueberries
- 150g (4½ ounces) blackberries
- 2 small fresh figs (100g), cut into wedges
- ½ cup (75g) cherries
- ¼ cup edible flowers, optional

1 Place dried figs in a small bowl with the water; stand for at least 2 hours. Drain figs; discard liquid.

2 Blend drained figs in a high-powered blender with almond milk, vanilla powder, syrup and rind until smooth. Transfer mixture to a medium bowl; whisk in seeds until combined.

3 Pour mixture into four ¾-cup (180ml) glasses, bowls or dishes. Cover, refrigerate for at least 2 hours or overnight.

4 Blend yoghurt and half of the blueberries until smooth: spoon evenly among glasses.

5 Serve puddings topped with blackberries, remaining blueberries, fresh figs, and cherries. Sprinkle with extra zested orange rind, extra chia seeds and edible flowers, if you like.

TIP To make orange zest to decorate, use a zester to remove the rind from half an orange. (Or, peel rind thinly from orange using a vegetable peeler, remove any white pith; cut rind into long thin strips.)

DO-AHEAD Puddings are best made the night before serving. They will keep for up to 3 days in the fridge.

SERVING IDEAS Decorate these puddings with heart-shaped chocolates.

Bircher muesli bowl

BIRCHER MUESLI WAS CREATED AT THE TURN OF THE CENTURY BY A SWISS DOCTOR WHO ESPOUSED EATING A DIET OF 50 PERCENT RAW FOODS FOR GOOD HEALTH.

- 3 cups (750ml) almond milk
- 1 tablespoon organic green tea leaves with coconut (see tip)
- 1 cup (90g) rolled oats
- ½ cup (100g) quinoa flakes
- 2 tablespoons black chia seeds
- 2 medium red apples (300g), grated coarsely
- 2 tablespoons pure maple syrup
- 1 medium red apple (150g), extra, sliced thinly
- ¼ small papaya (165g), seeds removed, peeled, cut into 1cm (½-inch) thick slices, then 3cm (1-inch) stars
- ½ cup (80g) natural or activated almonds, chopped coarsely
- ¼ cup edible flowers, optional

1 Heat milk in a medium saucepan until almost simmering. Remove from heat. Stir in tea; stand for 5 minutes. Strain mixture over a large heatproof bowl; discard tea leaves.

2 Add rolled oats, quinoa flakes, chia seeds and grated apple to bowl; stir to combine. Cover; refrigerate for 3 hours or overnight.

3 Before serving, drizzle maple syrup over bircher muesli; top with sliced apple, papaya, almonds and edible flowers.

TIP You can find green tea flavoured with coconut in the hot beverage section of major supermarkets, alternatively you can use regular green tea leaves.

DO-AHEAD You can keep the bircher muesli for 2 days, covered, in the fridge.

SERVING IDEAS Serve with vegan yoghurt (see page 40).

Baked porridge with stone fruit

WHILE BAKED PORRIDGE TAKES LONGER TO COOK, IT IS STILL CONVENIENT AS IT COOKS WITHOUT STIRRING OR TENDING AND REWARDS WITH A DELICIOUS CREAMINESS.

- 1½ cups (135g) rolled oats
- ½ cup (40g) desiccated coconut
- ½ teaspoon ground cinnamon
- ½ teaspoon ground ginger
- pinch sea salt
- ¼ cup (90g) pure maple syrup
- 1 teaspoon vanilla extract
- 3 cups (750ml) rice milk
- 2 stems rhubarb (125g), cut into 4cm lengths
- 3 medium plums (350g), halved
- 2 medium nectarines or peaches (340g), cut into thick wedges
- 2 tablespoons coconut sugar
- ⅓ cup (80ml) water
- edible flowers, to serve

1 Preheat oven to 180°C/350°F. Grease a 1.25 litre (5-cup) ovenproof dish.

2 Combine oats, coconut, cinnamon, ginger, salt, maple syrup and vanilla in an ovenproof dish; stir in milk. Pour mixture into ovenproof dish.

3 Bake for 40 minutes or until oats are tender and creamy.

4 Meanwhile, place rhubarb and stone fruit in a small baking dish. Sprinkle with coconut sugar and the water. Bake on a separate shelf, with porridge, for the last 20 minutes of porridge cooking time.

5 Serve porridge topped with baked fruit, fruit syrup and edible flowers, if you like.

TIP You can also use soy, almond or coconut milk.

SERVING IDEAS In winter, try roast pears and rhubarb instead of the stone fruit. Firm pears may take a little longer to cook. Serve with coconut yoghurt or vegan yoghurt (see page 40).

Blueberry pie brekkie pops

HAVE A BATCH OF THESE POPS IN YOUR FREEZER AT THE READY FOR BREAKFAST ON THE RUN, FOR HOT SUMMER MORNINGS, OR FOR A COOLING POST-WORKOUT SNACK.

- **250g (8 ounces) fresh or frozen blueberries**
- **1 teaspoon ground cinnamon**
- **⅓ cup (80ml) pure maple syrup**
- **½ teaspoon finely grated lemon rind**
- **1½ cups (180g) unrefined sugar muesli**
- **1 cup (250g) vegan coconut yoghurt**

1 Stir blueberries, cinnamon and 2 tablespoons of the syrup in a small saucepan over high heat; bring to the boil. Reduce heat to medium; simmer, mashing blueberries occasionally with a wooden spoon, for 5 minutes or until liquid is thickened slightly. Stir in rind. Transfer to a small bowl; refrigerate for 20 minutes or until cooled slightly.

2 Meanwhile, blend or process muesli until it resembles fine crumbs. Transfer to a small bowl, stir in remaining syrup.

3 Fold muesli mixture and yoghurt through blueberry mixture. Spoon yoghurt mixture into eight ⅓ cup (80ml) popsicle moulds, pressing down firmly.

4 Freeze pops for 2 hours or until firm enough to hold sticks upright. Insert sticks, making sure the sticks are centred.

5 Freeze popsicles for a further 4 hours or overnight until firm.

TIPS You can use your favourite muesli for this recipe. If you are having difficulty unmoulding popsicles, dip the moulds in warm water for 5 seconds to loosen.

Peanut butter & maple syrup crunch

GOLDEN LINSEEDS (FLAXSEEDS) ARE ONE OF THE RICHEST SOURCES OF HEART HEALTHY OMEGA-3 FATTY ACIDS AND MAY HELP IN THE PREVENTION OF SOME CANCERS.

- ⅓ cup (95g) smooth natural peanut butter
- ¼ cup (50g) coconut oil
- ¼ cup (90g) pure maple syrup
- 1 teaspoon vanilla bean paste
- 1½ cups (135g) rolled oats
- 1½ cups (150g) rolled barley
- ¼ cup (50g) amaranth
- ⅓ cup (65g) pepitas (pumpkin seed kernels)
- 2 tablespoons golden linseeds (flaxseeds)
- ⅓ cup (45g) chopped roasted salted peanuts

1 Preheat oven to 160°C/325°F. Line two oven trays with baking paper.

2 Stir peanut butter, coconut oil, maple syrup and vanilla paste in a small saucepan, over low heat until melted and smooth.

3 Combine oats, barley and amaranth in a large bowl; pour in peanut butter mixture, stir until combined. Spread between trays in an even layer.

4 Bake for 20 minutes, stirring once. Stir in pepitas and linseeds; bake for a further 30 minutes, stirring every 10 minutes, or until golden. Stir in peanuts; cool on trays. Store in an airtight container.

SWAP You can replace rolled barley with extra rolled oats. You can replace the amaranth with chia seeds.

DO-AHEAD The crunch will keep in an airtight glass jar or container for up to 1 month.

SERVING IDEA Serve topped with coconut yoghurt, apple, raspberries, nut or soy milk, then drizzled with extra maple syrup.

Food to go

Beetroot & za'atar dip with pitta chips

ZA'ATAR IS A MIDDLE EASTERN SPICE BLEND, WHICH GENERALLY INCLUDES THYME, SESAME SEEDS, SUMAC AND CUMIN IN EQUAL PROPORTIONS, WITH A LITTLE SALT.

- **3 large beetroots (beets) (600g)**
- **¼ cup (60ml) olive oil**
- **2 large wholemeal pittas (200g)**
- **1 tablespoon pepitas (pumpkin seed kernels)**
- **½ medium lemon (70g)**
- **⅔ cup (100g) roasted unsalted cashews**
- **¼ cup (70g) vegan yoghurt**
- **1½ teaspoons za'atar**
- **2 teaspoons olive oil, extra**

1 Preheat oven to 180°C/350°F.

2 Scrub beetroot well. Cut into 1cm (½-inch) cubes. Combine beetroot and 1 tablespoon of the oil on a large oven tray; season. Roast for 40 minutes; cool.

3 Meanwhile, cut bread into wedges. Place bread on two large oven trays; brush with remaining oil and season with sea salt. Bake for 10 minutes or until golden and crisp, turning over halfway through cooking. Spread pepitas onto a medium oven tray; roast for 5 minutes.

4 Remove rind from lemon using a zester (or peel rind thinly from lemon, avoiding white pith. Cut rind into long thin strips). Squeeze 1 tablespoon of juice from lemon.

5 Reserve ¼ cup of the beetroot. Process remaining beetroot, using the pulse button, until finely chopped. Add cashews; process until fine. Add juice, yoghurt and 1 teaspoon of the za'atar; pulse until combined. Season to taste.

6 Transfer beetroot mixture to a bowl; drizzle with extra oil. Sprinkle with remaining za'atar; top with reserved beetroot, toasted pepitas and rind. Serve dip with pitta chips.

TIP You can also make bread chips from thinly cut bagels.

SERVING IDEAS Serve with raw vegetable sticks, such as carrot or radish. Top with pine nuts, chopped almonds or sunflower seeds instead of pepitas.

PREP + COOK TIME 10 MINUTES (+ OVERNIGHT REFRIGERATION) **SERVES** 4

Tofu 'fetta'

YOU WILL NEED TO START THIS RECIPE A DAY AHEAD.

Whisk ½ cup (125ml) soy milk, ⅓ cup (80ml) rice wine vinegar, 1 tablespoon lemon juice, 1 teaspoon dried oregano leaves, 1 clove crushed garlic and 2 teaspoons table salt in a large, shallow glass or ceramic dish. Add 375g (12 ounces) extra firm tofu, cubed; turn to coat. Spread tofu in a single layer on a plate; cover with plastic wrap, refrigerate overnight. Drain 'fetta' and use straightaway, or pat 'fetta' dry and place in a container with 1 teaspoon black peppercorns and approximately 2 cups (500ml) olive oil or enough oil to cover 'fetta'; seal. Alternatively you can add additonal flavours to the oil using one of our variations below to flavour the 'fetta'.

DO-AHEAD 'Fetta' can be kept refrigerated in an airtight container for up to 1 week.

olive Combine the olive oil and peppercorns with ¼ cup pitted and torn kalamata olives, 2 cloves flattened garlic and 2 sprigs rosemary.

chilli Omit peppercorns. Combine the olive oil with 1 thinly sliced fresh long red chilli, 1 thinly sliced shallot and 2 sprigs thyme.

lemon Combine the olive oil and peppercorns with 3 fresh or dried bay leaves and three wide strips of lemon peel.

Fried tempeh nasi goreng

TO MAKE THE NASI GORENG YOU CAN ALSO USE RED, BROWN OR LONG-GRAIN WHITE RICE INSTEAD OF BLACK RICE, OR ANY LEFTOVER COOKED RICE.

- 1½ cups (300g) medium-grain black rice
- 2½ cups (625ml) water
- ¼ cup (60ml) peanut oil
- 500g (1 pound) tempeh, crumbled finely
- 3 fresh long red chillies, seeded, sliced
- 5 shallots (125g), chopped finely
- 3 large cloves garlic, sliced
- 4cm (1½-inch) piece fresh ginger (20g), chopped finely
- ½ small green cabbage (450g), shredded finely
- 2 tablespoons peanut oil, extra
- ⅓ cup (80ml) kecap manis
- 2 medium limes (180g), cut into 4 cheeks, centres reserved
- 2 green onions (scallions), sliced thinly
- 1 cup (80g) bean sprouts
- ¼ cup chopped fresh coriander (cilantro) leaves
- ¼ cup loosely packed fresh coriander (cilantro) leaves, extra

1 Bring rice and the water to the boil in a medium saucepan. Cover; simmer for 20 minutes or until just tender. Remove from heat; stand, covered, for 5 minutes. Spread rice out on a large tray; refrigerate until cold.

2 Heat half the oil in a wok over a high heat. Stir-fry tempeh for 6 minutes or until golden; season during cooking. Remove tempeh from wok with a slotted spoon; drain on paper towel.

3 Reserve a quarter of the chilli for serving. Heat remaining oil in wok over high heat; stir-fry shallots and remaining chilli for 2 minutes or until soft. Add garlic and ginger; stir-fry until fragrant. Add cabbage; stir-fry for 3 minutes or until tender. Transfer mixture to a large bowl.

4 Heat extra oil in wok; stir-fry cooled rice for 4 minutes or until golden. Add kecap manis; stir-fry until combined.

5 Return cabbage mixture to wok; squeeze in juice from reserved lime centres. Toss through three-quarters each of the green onion and tempeh, then bean sprouts and chopped coriander. Season to taste.

6 Serve nasi goreng with remaining tempeh, reserved chilli, remaining green onion and extra coriander leaves. Top with lime cheeks or wedges.

TIPS Place bean sprouts in iced water for 5 minutes to refresh before using. You can use soy sauce with a little maple syrup or brown or coconut sugar if you don't have kecap manis.
SERVING IDEAS Serve with sriracha (hot chilli sauce) and cos lettuce leaves or quarters.

Avocado salad kale wraps

THESE GLUTEN-FREE KALE WRAPS CAN BE LAYERED WITH BAKING PAPER AND FROZEN IN AN AIRTIGHT CONTAINER OR FREEZER BAG FOR UP TO 2 MONTHS.

- 2 tablespoons pepitas (pumpkin seed kernels)
- 1 cup (280g) vegan yoghurt
- 3 teaspoons wasabi paste
- 16 butter lettuce leaves
- 1 lebanese cucumber (130g), peeled into ribbons
- 70g (2½ ounces) snow pea shoots, trimmed
- 1 large avocado (320g), halved, sliced
- 2 green onions (scallions), sliced thinly

KALE WRAPS
- 5 stems purple kale (200g), trimmed
- 2½ tablespoons vegan yoghurt
- 1½ tablespoons ground LSA (see tips)
- 1 cup (160g) chickpea flour (besan)
- ½ teaspoon xanthan gum
- cooking-oil spray

1 Make kale wraps.

2 Stir pepitas in a small dry frying pan over medium heat for 2 minutes.

3 Whisk yoghurt and wasabi in a small bowl until combined; season to taste.

4 Divide lettuce, cucumber, pea shoots, avocado and yoghurt mixture among wraps. Top with pepitas and green onion; roll up to enclose.

5 Serve immediately or wrap firmly in plastic wrap or foil to go.

kale wraps Pour boiling water over kale in a large heatproof bowl; stand for 1 minute, drain. Refresh in another bowl of iced water; drain. Place kale in a tea towel; squeeze out excess water. Process kale until finely chopped; return to large bowl. Add remaining ingredients, except oil spray; season. Mix with your hands to form a dough. Knead dough on lightly floured surface until smooth. Divide dough into 8 pieces; roll into balls. Cut two pieces of baking paper a little smaller than a large non-stick frying pan. Spray paper with cooking oil then roll out a ball between greased baking paper.

Heat a large frying pan over a medium heat. As the wrap is very thin and fragile, peel one side of the paper away then place the wrap in the pan, paper-side up; cook for 30 seconds. Remove paper; turn wrap. Cook for a further 30 seconds. Repeat with remaining dough; cool.

TIPS LSA is a ground mixture of linseeds (L), sunflower seeds (S) and almonds (A). The wraps can be used in place of tortillas for burritos or soft tacos.

SAUCE VARIATIONS
Omit the wasabi in step 3 and instead combine the yoghurt with one of the following ingredients for different sauces:
BEETROOT Combine yoghurt and 2 teaspoons finely grated beetroot.
SPIRULINA Combine yoghurt and 1 teaspoon spirulina.
TURMERIC Combine yoghurt and 1 teaspoon ground turmeric.

Everday vegan mayo

THIS MAYO RECIPE IS DAIRY, EGG AND SOY-FREE.

Soak 1 cup (160g) whole blanched almonds for 4 hours; drain. Rinse under cold water; drain. Blend almonds with ½ cup (125ml) water until smooth. Add 1 tablespoon apple cider vinegar, 1 tablespoon lemon juice and 1 teaspoon dijon mustard; blend until smooth and combined. Season to taste. With motor operating, add ½ cup (125ml) olive oil in a slow, steady stream until smooth and combined. Store in an airtight container in the fridge for up to 1 month.

TIP You can add some crushed garlic to the mayonnaise to make an aïoli.

wasabi mayo Make everyday vegan mayo above; stir in 2 teaspoons wasabi paste or 1-2 teaspoons matcha powder. Serve with vegan sushi and other Asian inspired recipes.

chilli baconnaise Make everyday vegan mayo above; stir in 1 teaspoon smoked paprika, 2 teaspoons tomato paste, 1 clove crushed garlic and ¼ teaspoon chilli flakes. Serve with vegan burgers and anything that you'd like to add a little kick of smoky chilli flavour to.

turmeric mayo Make everyday vegan mayo above; stir in ½ teaspoon ground turmeric, 2 tablespoons finely grated carrot, 2 tablespoons white (shiro) miso and 1 tablespoon sesame oil. Works well with most things!

Red rice inside-out roll

FOR A NOURISHING MEAL SERVE THE ROLLS WITH STEAMED EDAMAME AND A BOWL OF MISO SOUP.

You will need a bamboo sushi mat for this recipe.

- 1½ cups (280g) red rice
- 3 cups (750ml) water
- ¼ cup (60ml) sushi seasoning
- 4 sheets nori
- 1 large beetroot (beet) (200g), peeled, cut into matchsticks
- 6 radishes (210g), cut into matchsticks
- 1 large carrot (180g), peeled, cut into matchsticks
- 2 lebanese cucumbers (260g), cut into matchsticks
- 1 large avocado (320g), cut into matchsticks
- tamari, wasabi paste, pickled ginger, for serving

1 Rinse rice in a sieve; drain well. Add rice and the water to a medium saucepan; bring to the boil. Reduce heat; simmer, covered, for 35 minutes or until rice is tender and breaks down a little. Overcooking the rice slightly will help the sushi to hold together. Spoon rice into a large bowl; stir in sushi seasoning with a fork. Season to taste with a little salt; cool.

2 Place sushi mat on a bench. Keep a bowl of iced water to dip your fingers in to stop the rice sticking. Place a sheet of nori close to the bottom edge of the mat. Press one quarter of the rice mixture firmly onto the nori, spreading thinly and leaving no borders. Turn nori rice-side down on mat; press firmly to even out rice. Add one quarter of the beetroot, radish, carrot, cucumber and avocado in a horizontal line in the bottom third of the nori, leaving a little poking out each end.

3 To roll, fold the bottom edge of the mat over the line of vegetables and press into a roll firmly, then continue rolling to finish. Roll the sushi in the mat between your hands a few times to make sure it's well formed. Wipe mat clean; repeat with remaining ingredients to make four rolls.

4 Cut each roll into six pieces. Serve on a platter with tamari, wasabi and pickled ginger.

TIPS Make sushi a few hours ahead of time and cut when you're ready to serve. You can also use regular sushi rice.

Cauliflower rig 'n' cheese

YOU CAN USE REGULAR OR GLUTEN-FREE PENNE, MACARONI, OR OTHER SHORT PASTA FOR THIS RECIPE.

You will need to start this recipe at least 4 hours ahead.

- **1 small cauliflower (1kg), cut into small florets**
- **2 tablespoons olive oil**
- **1 teaspoon garam masala**
- **1 fresh small red chilli, seeded, chopped finely, optional**
- **350g (11 ounces) rigatoni pasta**
- **⅓ cup torn fresh flat-leaf parsley**

CASHEW CHEESE SAUCE

- **2 cups (300g) raw cashews**
- **2 tablespoons olive oil**
- **2 medium onions (300g), chopped**
- **2 stalks celery (300g), trimmed, chopped**
- **⅔ cup (70g) nutritional yeast flakes (see Vegan Pantry, page 9)**
- **2 teaspoons wholegrain mustard**
- **1½ cups (375ml) oat milk or cashew nut milk (see tips)**

1 Make cashew cheese sauce.

2 Preheat grill (broiler). Place cauliflower, oil, garam masala and chilli in a medium bowl; toss to combine. Season. Spread cauliflower on an oven tray; place under grill for 15 minutes or until soft and golden, stirring occasionally.

3 Meanwhile, cook pasta in a large saucepan of boiling salted water until just tender; drain.

4 Combine cauliflower, pasta, half the parsley and half the cashew cheese sauce in a large bowl. Spoon into an 18cm x 23cm (7¼-inch x 9¼-inch) ovenproof dish. Spoon over remaining sauce. Grill for 4 minutes or until golden. Serve pasta topped with remaining parsley.

cashew cheese sauce Place cashews in a medium bowl; cover with filtered water. Stand, covered, for 4 hours or overnight. Drain cashews, rinse under cold water; drain well. Heat oil in a medium frying pan over medium heat; cook onion and celery, stirring, for 8 minutes or until soft. Add to a high-powered blender with cashews and remaining ingredients; blend until smooth. Season to taste.

TIPS You can use macadamias, almonds or brazil nuts instead of cashews.
Avoid using almond milk in this recipe as it can curdle on heating.
DO-AHEAD This dish can be covered tightly with plastic wrap, then foil and frozen for up to 1 month.
SERVING IDEAS Serve with a crisp green leafy salad with lemon dressing and warm garlic bread.

Chickpea pancakes with spicy baked beans

CHICKPEA FLOUR HAS A WONDERFUL NUTTY TASTE. THE TRICK WHEN ADDING THE WATER TO THE FLOUR IS TO ENSURE THAT IT IS COOL FROM THE TAP, NOT HOT.

- 1 cup (260g) hummus
- 2 canned chipotle chillies in adobo sauce
- 2 cups (300g) chickpea flour (besan)
- 1 teaspoon baking powder
- 1 teaspoon garlic powder
- 2 cups (500ml) water
- ¼ cup (60ml) olive oil
- 80g (2½ ounces) kale leaves, sliced thinly
- 2 x 420g (13½-ounce) cans baked beans
- 1 tablespoon mexican spice mix or chilli powder
- 2 medium avocados (500g), sliced thinly
- 4 radishes (140g), sliced thinly
- ½ cup loosely packed coriander (cilantro) sprigs
- 1 medium lime (65g), cut into wedges

1 Blend or process hummus and chilli until combined.

2 Whisk chickpea flour and powders in a medium bowl until well combined. Make a well in the centre; add water, whisk until mixture is smooth. Season.

3 Heat 1 tablespoon of the oil in a large non-stick frying pan over medium heat; cook kale, stirring, for 2 minutes or until wilted. Remove from pan; cover to keep kale warm.

4 Heat another 2 teaspoons of the oil in same pan. Add a quarter of the pancake mixture; cook for 2 minutes each side or until light golden. Transfer to a plate; cover to keep warm. Repeat with remaining oil and pancake mixture to make 4 pancakes in total.

5 Meanwhile, stir baked beans and spice mix in a small saucepan over low heat until hot.

6 Serve pancakes topped with hummus mixture, baked beans, avocado, kale, radish, coriander and lime wedges.

TIPS You can use spinach, baby spinach or silver beet (swiss chard) in place of the kale. The beans can be heated in the microwave.

DO-AHEAD Pancakes are best made on the day of serving.

Spiced white bean & greek salad pitta

USE OUR RECIPE TO MAKE YOUR OWN TOFU 'FETTA' (PAGE 62) OR USE A STORE BOUGHT VEGAN CHEESE SUBSTITUTE, IF YOU LIKE.

- ¼ cup (60ml) olive oil
- 1 small red onion (100g), chopped finely
- 1 clove garlic, crushed
- ¼ teaspoon dried oregano leaves
- 2 teaspoons ground cumin
- 400g (12½ ounces) canned cannellini beans, drained, rinsed (see tip)
- 1 tablespoon lemon juice
- 1 tablespoon chopped fresh flat-leaf parsley
- 4 wholemeal pocket pittas (420g)
- ⅓ cup (100g) vegan mayo (see page 70)
- ¼ cup (40g) pitted kalamata olives, halved
- 2 baby cucumbers (120g), quartered lengthways
- 8 golden cherry tomatoes, halved
- 1 cup (250g) tofu 'fetta' (see page 62)
- 1 medium lemon (140g), cut into wedges

1 Heat oil in a large frying pan over medium heat; cook onion, stirring, for 3 minutes or until softened. Increase heat to high. Add garlic, oregano, cumin and beans; cook, stirring, for 2 minutes or until lightly browned. Add juice and parsley; season to taste.

2 Meanwhile, warm pitta following packet directions.

3 Spread pitta with mayo. Combine olives, cucumber, tomatoes and tofu 'fetta' in a medium bowl. Spoon into pockets with warm bean mixture.

4 Serve pitta with lemon wedges.

TIP Save the drained liquid from the canned beans, called aquafaba, to use in meringues (see page 208). You can store it in the fridge for 2 days or freeze for up to 3 months.

TO GO To transport, pack pitta, mayo and salad separately and assemble just before serving.

Basic dressings

THESE THREE USEFUL VEGAN DRESSINGS CAN BE USED TO BOOST THE FLAVOUR OF ANY SIMPLE DISH, SUCH AS GREEN LEAFY SALADS OR COLD NOODLE BOWLS.

peanut dressing Whisk ⅓ cup (45g) coarsely chopped roasted unsalted peanuts, 1 thinly sliced green onion (scallion), 1 thinly sliced fresh long red chilli, 1 teaspoon finely grated fresh ginger, 1 clove crushed garlic, 1½ tablespoons grated palm sugar, 2 tablespoons sesame oil, 2 tablespoons tamari, ¼ cup (60ml) rice vinegar and 1½ tablespoons lime juice in a medium bowl until combined. (Makes 1¼ cups)

green goddess tahini yoghurt Process 1 small clove crushed garlic, 2 tablespoons lemon juice, 2 tablespoons tahini, ¾ cup (200g) vegan coconut yoghurt, 1 tablespoon shredded fresh flat-leaf parsley and 1 coarsely chopped medium (250g) avocado until smooth and well combined; season to taste. (Makes 1¾ cups)

ginger-turmeric dressing Heat ½ cup (125ml) olive oil in a small frying pan over low heat; cook 1 seeded, thinly sliced fresh long red chilli, 2 thinly sliced cloves garlic, 2 teaspoons finely chopped fresh ginger, 1 teaspoon crushed coriander seeds, and ½ teaspoon ground turmeric, stirring, for 1 minute or until fragrant. Remove from heat; stir in ⅓ cup (80ml) white wine vinegar. (Makes ¾ cup)

Pea & edamame toasts with avocado & umeboshi plum

UMEBOSHI PLUMS ARE REGARDED FOR THEIR HEALTH BENEFITS, WHICH MAY INCLUDE REDUCING FATIGUE, STIMULATING DIGESTION AND ELIMINATING TOXINS.

- 1 cup (100g) frozen edamame (soybean) pods
- 1 cup (120g) frozen peas
- ½ cup loosely packed fresh mint leaves
- 1 tablespoon lemon juice
- 2 tablespoons olive oil
- 4 slices sourdough bread (185g), toasted
- 2 tablespoons olive oil, extra
- 1 tablespoon umeboshi plum paste (see tips)
- 1 small avocado (200g), sliced
- 2 watermelon radishes (70g), trimmed, sliced thinly
- 1 tablespoon micro herbs

1 Add edamame to a medium saucepan of boiling water; cook for 2 minutes. Add frozen peas; cook for a further 2 minutes or until tender. Drain; rinse under cold water. Shell edamame; discard pods.

2 Process edamame, peas and mint until combined but still chunky. Add juice and a little of the oil. With motor operating, gradually add remaining oil in a thin stream until a spreadable consistency. Transfer to a small bowl; season to taste.

3 Brush the bread with extra oil. Toast bread on heated grill plate (or grill or barbecue) over high heat until browned. Spread toast with plum paste and pea mixture. Top with avocado, radish and herbs and season. Drizzle with a little more olive oil, if you like.

TIP Umeboshi plum paste is available from Japanese food stores and some health food stores. If you can't find umeboshi plum paste, use seasoned Japanese plum (shiraboshiume). Remove skin and seed, then mash the pulp.

DO-AHEAD The pea mixture can be made several hours ahead. Prepare from step 3 just before serving.

Roast pumpkin, leek & fig tart

SOME CARAMELISED BALSAMIC VINEGARS CONTAIN LACTOSE. CHECK THE INGREDIENTS LIST FIRST TO MAKE SURE THE BRAND YOU USE IS DAIRY-FREE.

- 500g (1 pound) kent pumpkin, cut into 2cm (¾-inch) thick wedges
- 2 tablespoons fresh rosemary leaves
- 1½ tablespoons olive oil
- 1 large leek (500g), sliced
- 2 teaspoons balsamic vinegar
- 4 medium fresh figs (240g), sliced
- 2 tablespoons pepitas (pumpkin seed kernels), toasted
- 1 tablespoon caramelised balsamic vinegar

PASTRY
- 1½ cups (225g) chickpea flour (besan)
- ½ cup (75g) buckwheat flour
- 1 teaspoon sea salt
- ¼ cup (60ml) olive oil
- ⅓ cup (80ml) cold water, approximately

1 Preheat oven to 220°C/450°F. Line two oven trays with baking paper.
2 Make pastry.
3 Place pumpkin, rosemary and half the oil on an oven tray; toss to coat. Roast for 30 minutes or until golden and tender. Reduce oven to 200°C/400°F.
4 Meanwhile, heat remaining oil in a medium frying pan over medium heat; cook leek, stirring, for 8 minutes or until soft. Add vinegar; cook for a further 3 minutes or until sticky and caramelised. Spoon leek mixture onto pastry. Top with roasted pumpkin.
5 Bake tart for 20 minutes or until topping starts to caramelise and pastry is golden. Serve topped with figs and pepitas; drizzle with caramelised balsamic vinegar.

pastry Sift flours and salt into a medium bowl; add oil and the water. Use a round-bladed knife to "cut" through the flour mixture until it forms a dough. Roll pastry a on lightly floured bench to a 25cm x 30cm (10-inch x 12-inch) oval. If the dough is too sticky, knead in a little extra flour. Transfer pastry to remaining oven tray.

TIPS To toast the pepitas, spread onto an oven tray. Toast for 5 minutes, or until browned lightly. Or, place seeds in a heavy-based frying pan, stir over medium heat until browned lightly.

The botanist burger

THIS RECIPE PROVES THAT A FABULOUS VEGAN BURGER, SAUCE AND 'CHIPS' REALLY CAN BE CONSTRUCTED SOLELY FROM PLANT-BASED FOOD.

- 800g (1½ pounds) canned chickpeas (garbanzo beans), drained, rinsed (see tip)
- 2 tablespoons chickpea flour (besan)
- ⅔ cup firmly packed fresh flat-leaf parsley leaves
- 1 cup firmly packed fresh mint leaves
- 2 teaspoons finely grated lemon rind
- 6 green onions (scallions), chopped finely
- ½ cup (125g) vegan mayo (see page 70)
- 2 cloves garlic, crushed
- 2 tablespoons finely chopped fresh chives
- 2 medium zucchini (240g), sliced thinly lengthways
- 4 sourdough seeded bread rolls, halved, toasted
- 2 small avocados (400g), sliced
- 2 cups (80g) firmly packed fresh watercress leaves

KALE CHIPS
- 250g (8 ounces) kale
- 1 tablespoon olive oil

1 Make kale chips.

2 Meanwhile, process chickpeas, flour, parsley, mint and rind until mixture comes together. Transfer to a medium bowl; stir in green onion, season to taste. Shape mixture into four patties. Place on a plate; refrigerate for 20 minutes.

3 Process mayo, garlic and chives in a clean food processor bowl until combined.

4 Cook zucchini on heated oiled grill plate (or grill or barbecue) over medium-high heat for 2 minutes each side or until tender. Transfer to a plate; cover to keep warm.

5 Cook patties on same oiled grill plate for 2 minutes each side or until browned and heated through.

6 Spoon mayo mixture on base of rolls; top with patties, zucchini, avocado and watercress, then roll tops. Serve with kale chips.

kale chips Preheat oven to 180°C/350°F. Line two oven trays with baking paper. Remove stems from kale; tear leaves into medium-size pieces. Place in a large bowl with oil. Massage the oil into kale, place kale a single layer on trays. Bake for 10 minutes. Rotate trays; bake for a further 5 minutes or until kale is crisp. Cool. Season to taste.

TIP You can save the drained liquid, called aquafaba, from the canned chickpeas. It can be used to make vegan meringues (see page 208), or mousse (see page 211). Store aquafaba in the fridge for 2 days in a container or frozen for up to 3 months.
DO-AHEAD Patties can be made a day ahead; keep covered in the fridge. Or, wrap individually in plastic wrap and freeze in an airtight container for up to 2 months.

Satay tofu & roast pumpkin wraps

TOFU AND PUMPKIN CAN BE EATEN WARM IF EATING IMMEDIATELY; IF YOU'RE MAKING IT TO GO, COOL BEFORE PLACING INSIDE THE WRAPS.

- ¼ cup (60ml) coconut milk
- 1 tablespoon crunchy peanut butter
- 1 teaspoon tamari
- 400g (12½ ounces) satay tofu, cut into 3cm (1¼-inch) thick rectangles
- 400g (12½ ounces) pumpkin, peeled, cut into 1.5cm (1-inch) thick slices
- 1 tablespoon olive oil
- 4 spinach and herb wraps (282g)
- 1 gem or cos (romaine) lettuce, trimmed, whole or shredded
- 1 cup (80g) finely shredded red cabbage
- 100g (3 ounces) snow peas, trimmed, cut into matchsticks
- 1 medium red capsicum (bell pepper) (150g), sliced thinly
- 1 medium yellow capsicum (bell pepper) (150g), sliced thinly
- 1 medium beetroot (beet) (150g), peeled, cut into matchsticks
- 1 medium avocado (250g), sliced thinly

1 Preheat oven to 200°C/400°F. Line two oven trays with baking paper.
2 Combine coconut milk, peanut butter and tamari in a medium bowl. Dip tofu pieces in mixture to coat; place on one tray.
3 Place pumpkin and oil on remaining tray; season. Roast tofu and pumpkin for 20 minutes, turning halfway or until golden.
4 Place wraps on a clean bench. Divide lettuce, cabbage, snow peas, capsicum, beetroot, tofu, roast pumpkin and avocado among wraps. Roll up tightly; cut in half.

TIPS Make these into rice paper rolls by substituting rice paper wrappers for the bread wraps. Cut the pumpkin and tofu into smaller pieces and use at least 8 rounds of rice paper.
ADD-ONS If you would like extra sauce with these try our peanut dressing (see page 80) or serve with green goddess tahini yoghurt (see page 80).
Scatter with coriander sprigs and fresh mint leaves, if you like.
TO GO To transport, wrap in baking paper then firmly in plastic wrap.

kale, orange & toasted mixed seed salad

THE IRON IN PLANT FOODS LIKE KALE IS NOT AS WELL ABSORBED AS THAT IN MEAT, BUT EATEN WITH VITAMIN C-RICH FOODS LIKE CITRUS, THE UPTAKE IS INCREASED.

- 1 medium blood orange (240g)
- 2 tablespoons sunflower seeds
- 2 tablespoons pepitas (pumpkin seed kernels)
- 1 tablespoon black sesame seeds
- 250g (8 ounces) kale
- 1 tablespoon olive oil
- 400g (12½ ounces) canned chickpeas (garbanzo beans), drained, rinsed

ORANGE & TAHINI DRESSING
- ¼ cup (60ml) hulled tahini
- ¼ cup (60ml) warm water, approximately

1 Finely grate rind from orange; reserve 1 teaspoon for the dressing. Segment orange by peeling rind thickly from orange so no white pith remains. Cut between membranes, over a bowl to catch juice, releasing segments into another bowl. Squeeze juice from membranes; you will need 2 tablespoons juice for the dressing.

2 Make orange and tahini dressing.

3 Place seeds in a small frying pan; stir seeds continuously over medium heat for 2 minutes or until they are lightly browned. Transfer to a small bowl.

4 Remove stems from kale; shred kale finely. Place kale in a large bowl with oil; rub oil into kale until leaves begin to soften.

5 Add chickpeas, orange segments and dressing to kale; toss gently to combine. Serve sprinkled with toasted seeds. Season.

orange & tahini dressing Whisk tahini with reserved rind and juice in a small bowl. Gradually add enough of the water until dressing becomes a pouring consistency; whisk until smooth. Season to taste.

DO-AHEAD Orange & tahini dressing can be made 2 hours ahead but will thicken on standing; whisk in a little extra cold water or orange juice before serving.

Crisp Tofu bánh mì

USE A MANDOLINE OR V-SLICER TO MAKE SHORT WORK OF CUTTING THE VEGETABLES INTO MATCHSTICKS.

- 1 medium carrot (120g), cut into matchsticks
- 1 small lebanese cucumber (100g), halved, seeded, cut into batons
- 3 trimmed red radishes (45g), sliced thinly
- ½ cup (125ml) rice wine vinegar
- 1 tablespoon coconut sugar
- ½ teaspoon salt
- ⅓ cup (100g) vegan mayo (see page 70)
- ⅓ cup loosely packed fresh coriander (cilantro) leaves
- 1 fresh long green chilli, sliced thinly
- ⅓ cup (50g) cornflour (cornstarch)
- 300g (9½ ounces) firm tofu, cut into 8 long slices
- 2 tablespoons olive oil
- 4 long wholegrain sourdough bread rolls (200g), split (see tips)
- 1½ cups (120g) shredded red cabbage
- hot chilli sauce, to taste
- ½ cup loosely packed fresh coriander (cilantro) leaves, extra
- ½ cup loosely packed fresh mint leaves

1 Place carrot, cucumber and radish in a medium bowl. Pour vinegar over vegetables; sprinkle with coconut sugar and salt. Stir to combine.

2 Blend or process mayo, coriander and half the fresh chilli until smooth.

3 Place cornflour on a plate. Toss tofu in cornflour to coat. Heat oil in a large frying pan over medium-high heat. Cook tofu, turning, until golden and heated through.

4 Drain vegetables; reserve pickling liquid for another use (see tips).

5 Divide cabbage, pickled vegetables, tofu, mayo mixture, chilli sauce, extra coriander, mint and remaining fresh chilli between bread rolls.

TIPS Check the bread rolls are free from dairy products. The leftover pickling liquid can be used in place of vinegar in salad dressings; keep refrigerated in a glass jar for several months.

Roast carrot & garlic soup with crunchy chickpeas

IF YOU USE ORGANIC CARROTS, GIVE THEM A WASH, BUT DON'T PEEL AS THE SKIN IS HIGH IN PHYTONUTRIENTS. OTHERWISE, IT'S BEST TO PEEL THEM FIRST.

- 1kg (2 pounds) carrots, chopped coarsely
- 2 medium onions (300g), chopped coarsely
- ¼ cup (60ml) olive oil
- 1 teaspoon cumin seeds
- ¼ teaspoon dried chilli flakes
- 1 bulb garlic, halved
- ¼ cup (30g) rinsed chickpeas (garbanzo beans)
- 3 teaspoons za'atar
- 1.5 litres (6 cups) water
- ½ cup small fresh coriander (cilantro) leaves

1 Preheat oven to 200°C/400°F. Line two oven trays with baking paper.

2 Divide carrot and onion between the trays. Drizzle with 2 tablespoons of the oil; sprinkle with seeds and chilli. Season. Roast for 30 minutes. Add garlic to a tray; roast for a further 15 minutes or until vegetables and garlic are tender.

3 Meanwhile, place chickpeas on a shallow-sided oven tray; drizzle with remaining oil. Sprinkle with za'atar; toss to coat. Roast for 10 minutes or until fragrant and browned lightly.

4 Squeeze garlic from skin; discard skin. Transfer vegetables and garlic to a large saucepan; add the water. Bring to the boil over high heat. Reduce heat; simmer, uncovered, for 10 minutes. Stand 10 minutes.

5 Blend or process soup until smooth; season. Reheat soup gently if needed.

6 Serve soup topped with chickpeas and coriander.

DO-AHEAD Soup can be made up to 2 days ahead to the end of step 5; keep covered in the fridge. Keep roasted chickpeas in an airtight container at room temperature.
SERVING IDEAS Serve topped with a dollop of vegan yoghurt (see page 40).

Sprouted bread with dill-pea spread & fermented vegies

EATING FERMENTED FOODS ADDS LIVE MICROBES TO THE EXISTING COLONY OF MICROBES THAT LIVE IN OUR GUT, AND CONTRIBUTE TO GOOD AND BALANCED HEALTH.

- 3 cups (360g) frozen peas
- ⅓ cup (90g) hulled tahini
- 2 tablespoons fresh dill leaves
- 1 clove garlic, crushed
- 2 tablespoons lemon juice
- 1 tablespoon dijon mustard
- 2 tablespoons sunflower seeds
- 2 teaspoons sesame seeds
- 2 teaspoons linseeds (flaxseeds)
- 9 x 80g (1½ pounds total) slices sprouted bread (see tip)
- 1⅓ cups (240g) drained store-bought fermented vegetables of choice
- 1 cup (15g) loosely packed snow pea tendrils
- ½ medium lemon (70g), cut into 4 wedges

1 Place peas in a heatproof bowl; cover with boiling water. Stand for 2 minutes; drain. Blend or process peas, tahini, dill, garlic, juice and mustard until it forms a chunky spread. Season to taste.

2 Place seeds in a small heavy-based frying pan; stir seeds constantly over medium-high heat until browned lightly.

3 Top toasted bread with spread, vegetables, seeds and snow pea tendrils. Serve with lemon wedges.

TIP Sprouted bread is available from some health food stores, gourmet food stores and markets; keep refrigerated.

DO-AHEAD Pea spread can be kept in an airtight container in the fridge for up to 1 day. Toast the bread and assemble just before serving.

Savoury yoghurt & spicy chickpea jars

SERVE THESE SALAD JARS WITH CRISP BREAD OR CHARGRILLED SLICES OF WHOLEGRAIN BREAD.

- 2 cups (560g) vegan yoghurt
- ½ cup finely chopped fresh dill leaves
- 2 cloves garlic, crushed
- ½ cup (125ml) lemon juice
- 2 x 400g (12½ ounces) canned chickpeas (garbanzo beans), drained, rinsed (see tips)
- ⅓ cup (55g) currants
- 150g (4½ ounces) drained char-grilled capsicum (bell pepper), sliced thinly
- 1 small red onion (100g), quartered and sliced thinly
- 2 lebanese cucumbers (260g), chopped finely
- ½ cup (70g) slivered almonds, toasted
- 2 teaspoons harissa paste
- 2 tablespoons olive oil

1 Combine yoghurt, dill, half the garlic and 2 tablespoons of the juice in a small bowl. Season to taste.
2 Combine chickpeas, currants, capsicum, onion, cucumber and ⅓ cup of the almonds in a medium bowl.
3 Combine harissa, oil and remaining garlic and juice in a small bowl.
4 Spoon yoghurt mixture into four 1½ cup (375ml) jars. Top with salad and a spoonful of harissa dressing.

TIP You can save the drained liquid, called aquafaba, from the canned chickpeas. It can be used to make vegan meringues (see page 208), or mousse (see page 211). Store aquafaba in the fridge for 2 days in a container or frozen for up to 3 months.
SWAP Try other legumes in this recipe, such as white beans or four bean mix.

Daily greens skillet fillo pie

EAT MORE WIDELY BY ROTATING THE TYPES OF GREENS YOU EAT TO CAPTURE THE DIFFERENT VALUABLE NUTRITIONAL QUALITIES EACH PROVIDES.

- 750g (1½ pounds) silver beet (swiss chard)
- ¼ cup (60ml) olive oil
- 1 medium leek (350g), sliced thinly
- 3 cloves garlic, crushed
- 1 tablespoon white spelt plain (all-purpose) flour
- 1 cup (250ml) vegetable stock
- 2 medium zucchini (240g), cut into 1cm (½-inch) slices
- 200g (6½ ounces) broccolini, cut into 5cm (2-inch) lengths
- 1 cup (120g) frozen baby peas
- 6 sheets fillo pastry
- 2 teaspoons black sesame seeds
- 2 teaspoons white sesame seeds

1 Preheat oven to 220°C/425°F.

2 Trim ends of silver beet stems; chop stems into 1cm (½-inch) pieces. Coarsely shred leaves.

3 Heat 2 tablespoons of the oil in a 26cm (10½-inch) (base measurement) 27cm (10¾-inch) (top measurement) frying pan over medium heat. Cook leek and silver beet stems, stirring occasionally, for 7 minutes or until softened. Add garlic; cook, stirring, for 1 minute or until fragrant. Add flour; stir until combined. Gradually stir in stock; bring to the boil, simmer, uncovered, for 2 minutes or until liquid has thickened slightly.

4 Pour boiling water over shredded silver beet in a large heatproof bowl; stand for 1 minute, drain. Refresh in another bowl of iced water; drain. Squeeze out as much liquid as possible, then stir into leek mixture with zucchini, broccolini and peas. Season to taste. Cool for 20 minutes.

5 Brush fillo sheets with remaining oil, loosely scrunch sheets over the mixture in the pan; sprinkle with both seeds. Bake for 15 minutes or until pastry is golden. Stand pie for 10 minutes before serving.

TIPS This pie can be eaten hot, warm or cold. To take on a picnic, simply cool, wrap the frying pan in a clean tea towel and away you go! Make sure the pan or skillet is non-reactive, that is, not aluminium, pitted or with any rust spots. SERVING IDEAS Serve with lemon cheeks and vegan yoghurt (see page 40) or raw beetroot hummus (see page 140).

Miso peanut bowl with shredded winter veg

WE USE SHIRO MISO, ALSO KNOWN AS WHITE MISO; WHILE IT IS LIGHTER THAN OTHER TYPES, IT'S GOLDEN IN COLOUR.

- 1 baby fennel bulb (130g)
- 1 cup (80g) finely shredded red cabbage
- 1 cup (80g) finely shredded green cabbage
- 1 medium beetroot (beet) (150g), peeled, cut into matchsticks
- 400g (12½ ounces) baby carrots, trimmed, peeled into ribbons
- ⅓ cup (45g) finely chopped roasted unsalted peanuts
- ½ cup loosely packed fresh mint leaves
- 1 medium lime (90g), cut into wedges

MISO PEANUT DRESSING
- ½ cup (140g) crunchy natural peanut butter
- ¼ cup (70g) white (shiro) miso
- 2 tablespoons coconut sugar
- ½ teaspoon finely grated lime rind
- 1 fresh small red chilli, chopped finely
- ⅓ cup (80ml) lime juice
- ½ cup (125ml) water

1 Make miso peanut dressing.
2 Thinly slice fennel bulb and stems.
3 Divide fennel and remaining ingredients between bowls, top with peanuts and mint. Serve with dressing and lime wedges.

miso peanut dressing Blend or process ingredients until combined.

TIPS Use a mandoline or V-slicer for the vegetables for best results.
Toss the fennel in lime juice to prevent it from browning if not serving immediately.
Seed the chilli if you prefer less heat.
SERVING IDEA For a more substantial meal, you can add sliced teriyaki-flavoured or plain tofu.
TO GO When travelling, store the dressing and the salad ingredients separately; combine when serving.

Roasted cauliflower dip with rice crackers

YOU CAN USE PRECOOKED BROWN RICE FOR THIS RECIPE OR BOIL ABOUT ⅓ CUP (65G) RAW BROWN RICE.

- 400g (12½ ounces) cauliflower, cut into florets
- ¼ cup (60ml) olive oil
- 1 tablespoon hazelnut dukkah
- 3 cloves garlic, unpeeled
- ½ cup (140g) vegan yoghurt
- 400g (12½ ounces) canned cannellini beans, drained, rinsed
- 2 tablespoons lemon juice
- 2 tablespoons finely chopped fresh chives
- ¼ cup (35g) coarsely chopped roasted hazelnuts
- 1 tablespoon hazelnut dukkah, extra

RICE CRACKERS
- ¼ cup (45g) linseeds (flaxseeds)
- ⅓ cup (70g) red quinoa, rinsed
- 2 cups (500ml) water
- 1 cup (175g) cooked brown rice (see note above)
- 1 teaspoon sea salt
- 2 teaspoons tamari
- 1½ tablespoons olive oil
- ⅓ cup (50g) sesame seeds, toasted

1 Make rice crackers.

2 Preheat oven to 220°C/425°F. Line an oven tray with baking paper.

3 Place cauliflower on tray. Drizzle with half the oil; sprinkle with dukkah. Toss to coat. Add garlic to tray. Roast for 30 minutes or until tender. Cool to room temperature.

4 Process cauliflower, peeled garlic, yoghurt, beans, juice and remaining oil until smooth. Stir in chives. Season. Transfer to a serving bowl. Sprinkle with hazelnuts and extra dukkah.

5 Serve dip with crackers and crudités. Season to taste.

rice crackers Place linseeds in a small bowl; add enough water to cover. Stand for at least 20 minutes. Drain well; pat dry with paper towel. Meanwhile, place quinoa and the water in a small saucepan; bring to the boil. Simmer, uncovered, for 12 minutes or until tender. Drain well; cool. Blend or process linseeds, quinoa, rice, salt, tamari and oil in a food processor until mixture forms a ball; add 1 tablespoon of water, if needed. Add sesame seeds; pulse to combine. Dough will be very sticky. Preheat oven to 200°C/400°F. Divide dough in half. Roll each half between sheets of baking paper until 2mm (⅛-inch) thick. Remove top layer of baking paper. Using a knife, score top of dough into desired shapes; slide on paper onto oven trays. Bake for 40 minutes or until crisp and golden. Cool 5 minutes. Break crackers along score lines; cool.

DO-AHEAD Crackers can be made a week ahead. Store in an airtight container. SERVING IDEAS Crudités such as sliced cucumber, radishes and baby carrots.

Vegie patties with beetroot & caraway chutney

BEETROOT CHUTNEY CAN BE MADE UP TO A WEEK AHEAD. STORE IN AN AIRTIGHT CONTAINER IN THE FRIDGE

- ¾ cup (150g) millet
- 3 cups (750ml) water
- ¼ cup (60ml) olive oil
- 1 small onion (80g), chopped finely
- 1 clove garlic, crushed
- 2cm (¾-inch) piece fresh ginger (10g), grated
- 1 small orange sweet potato (250g), peeled, grated
- 1 cup (160g) frozen corn kernels
- 75g (2½ ounces) baby spinach leaves
- ¼ cup chopped fresh basil leaves
- ¾ cup (210g) hulled tahini
- ½ cup (60g) almond meal
- grapeseed oil, for shallow-frying
- 6 wholegrain bread rolls (300g)
- 100g (3½ ounces) salad leaves
- ½ cup (120g) cashew 'cheese'

BEETROOT & CARAWAY CHUTNEY

- 1 tablespoon olive oil
- 1 medium red onion (150g), chopped finely
- 2 teaspoons caraway seeds
- 2 medium beetroot (beets) (400g), grated coarsely
- ½ cup (125ml) apple cider vinegar
- ¾ cup (165g) raw sugar
- ¾ cup (180ml) coconut water

1 Make beetroot and caraway chutney.

2 Meanwhile, bring millet and the water to the boil in a medium saucepan. Reduce heat to medium; simmer, uncovered, for 15 minutes or until soft. Drain.

3 Heat olive oil in a large frying pan over medium heat; cook onion, garlic and ginger, stirring, for 5 minutes or until onion softens. Add sweet potato and corn; cook, stirring, for 5 minutes or until corn softens. Remove from heat; stir in spinach. Transfer to a medium bowl; stir in millet, basil, tahini and almond meal. Season to taste.

4 Shape mixture into 12 patties; place on a baking-paper-lined tray. Refrigerate for 30 minutes.

5 Heat grapeseed oil in a large frying pan over medium-high heat; shallow-fry patties, in batches, for 3 minutes each side or until golden. Drain patties on paper towel.

6 Serve vegie patties on bread rolls with salad leaves, cashew 'cheese' and chutney.

beetroot & caraway chutney Heat oil in medium saucepan over medium heat; cook onion and seeds, stirring, for 5 minutes or until onion softens. Add beetroot, vinegar, sugar and coconut water; bring to a simmer. Simmer, uncovered, over low-medium heat, for 45 minutes or until beetroot is soft and mixture is thickened. Season to taste. Cool.

Green couscous salad

YOU COULD ALSO USE WHOLEMEAL PEARL COUSCOUS FOR THIS RECIPE; IT'S AVAILABLE FROM SOME DELIS. FOLLOW COOKING DIRECTIONS ON PACKET.

- 1 cup (200g) wholemeal couscous
- 1 cup (250ml) boiling water
- 150g (4½ ounces) fresh podded peas (see tips)
- 200g (7 ounces) sugar snap peas, halved lengthways
- 3 green onions (scallions), sliced thinly
- 1 small green capsicum (bell pepper) (150g), sliced thinly
- 2 medium avocados (500g), sliced thinly
- ⅓ cup (45g) chopped pistachios
- ¼ cup loosely packed fresh dill sprigs
- ¼ cup loosely packed fresh coriander (cilantro) leaves
- ¼ cup loosely packed fresh mint leaves
- ¼ cup (60ml) lime juice
- ⅓ cup (80ml) olive oil
- 1 clove garlic, crushed
- ½ cup snow pea tendrils
- 1 lime, cut into wedges

1 Place couscous and the boiling water in a large heatproof bowl. Cover; stand for 5 minutes or until liquid is absorbed, fluffing with a fork occasionally.

2 Meanwhile, place peas and sugar snap peas in a medium heatproof bowl; add enough boiling water to cover. Stand for 1 minute, drain. Refresh in another bowl of iced water; drain.

3 Add peas to couscous with green onion, capsicum, avocado, half the pistachios and herbs in a large bowl.

4 Place juice, oil and garlic in a screw-top jar; shake well. Season to taste.

5 Add dressing to salad. Serve salad topped with snow pea tendrils, remaining pistachios and lime wedges.

TIPS Podded fresh peas are available from some greengrocers. If unavailable, you will need to buy about 300g (9½ ounces) peas in the pod.

To make an avocado "rose", cut a firm, ripe avocado in half, remove the seed and peel. Thinly slice one half at a time and fan it into a long line, with slices overlapping by two thirds. Cut towards the centre and squeeze over some lime or lemon juice to prevent browning.

TO GO If packing the salad, pack the salad, avocado and dressing separately. Quarter the avocado with the skin on. Remove the seed, then put it back into the centre of the avocado and re-assemble. Wrap it firmly in plastic wrap to prevent browning. Peel avocado just before serving. Or, place peeled avocado into a small airtight container; drizzle with plenty of lime or lemon juice, then slice before serving.

Broccoli arancini with rocket & almond pesto

GLUTEN-FREE BREADCRUMBS ARE AVAILABLE FROM SOME SUPERMARKETS AND HEALTH FOOD STORES. CHECK THE LABEL FOR ANY DAIRY PRODUCTS.

- **3 cups (750ml) vegetable stock**
- **2 tablespoons olive oil**
- **1 medium leek (350g), chopped finely**
- **1 clove garlic, crushed**
- **1 cup (200g) arborio rice**
- **1 cup (250ml) dry white wine**
- **150g (4½ ounces) broccoli, cut into small florets**
- **2 teaspoons finely grated lemon rind**
- **1½ cups (110g) packaged gluten-free breadcrumbs**
- **grapeseed oil, for deep-frying**

ROCKET & ALMOND PESTO

- **100g (3 ounces) rocket (arugula), chopped coarsely**
- **½ cup (80g) roasted almond kernels, chopped coarsely**
- **2 tablespoons nutritional yeast flakes (see Vegan Pantry, page 9)**
- **½ cup (125ml) olive oil**

1 Bring stock to the boil in a large saucepan. Reduce heat; simmer, covered.

2 Meanwhile, heat olive oil in a medium saucepan over medium heat; cook leek and garlic, stirring, for 2 minutes or until leek is soft. Reduce heat to low. Add rice; stir to coat in oil mixture. Add wine; cook, stirring, for 2 minutes or until wine is evaporated.

3 Stir in ½ cup of the hot stock; cook, stirring, over low heat until liquid is absorbed. Continue adding stock, in ½-cup batches, stirring, until liquid is absorbed after each addition. Total cooking time should be about 20 minutes or until rice is just tender, adding broccoli during last 10 minutes of cooking. Stir in rind; season to taste. Spread rice mixture over a large oven tray; cool for 15 minutes.

4 With wet hands, roll ¼-cups of rice mixture into balls. Toss balls in breadcrumbs to coat; place on a tray. Refrigerate for 30 minutes.

5 Meanwhile, make rocket and almond pesto.

6 Fill a large saucepan one-third full with grapeseed oil; heat to 180°C/350°F (or until a cube of bread turns golden in 15 seconds). Deep-fry balls, in batches, for 2 minutes, turning occasionally, until browned lightly and cooked through. Drain on paper towel.

7 Serve arancini with pesto.

rocket & almond pesto Process ingredients in a small food processor until almost smooth. Transfer to a small bowl; season to taste.

DO-AHEAD Recipe can be made to the end of step 5 a day ahead. Keep arancini covered in the fridge. Keep pesto in a small airtight container, with plastic wrap on the surface, in the fridge. SERVING IDEA Serve with a green leaf or tomato salad and lemon wedges.

Cavolo nero & lentil salad with tempeh chips

CAVOLO NERO IS ALSO KNOWN AS TUSCAN CABBAGE. YOU CAN USE OTHER LEAFY GREENS LIKE KALE, SILVER BEET (SWISS CHARD) OR SPINACH INSTEAD.

- 1¾ cups (350g) french-style dried green lentils
- 10 cavolo nero (tuscan cabbage) leaves (100g), trimmed, shredded
- 400g (12½ ounces) mixed cherry tomato medley, halved
- 1 small red onion (80g), quartered, sliced thinly
- ¼ cup loosely packed small fresh basil leaves
- ¼ cup loosely packed fresh mint leaves
- ¼ cup loosely packed fresh flat-leaf parsley leaves
- ½ cup (125ml) olive oil
- ¼ cup (60ml) red wine vinegar
- 2 teaspoons dijon mustard

TEMPEH CHIPS
- ¼ cup (60ml) olive oil
- 100g (3 ounces) tempeh, cut into 3mm (⅛-inch) slices

1 Cook lentils in a large saucepan of boiling water, uncovered, for 12 minutes or until just tender; drain. Rinse under cold water; drain well.

2 Meanwhile, make tempeh chips.

3 Arrange lentils, cavolo nero, tomato, onion and herbs on plates or trays.

4 Place oil, vinegar and mustard in a screw-top jar, shake well. Season to taste.

5 Serve salad with tempeh chips and dressing in small bowls to the side.

tempeh chips Heat oil in a large frying pan over medium-high heat; cook tempeh for 1 minute each side or until golden. Drain on paper towel.

TIPS French-style green lentils, grown in Australia, are related to the famous French lentils du puy; these green-blue, tiny lentils have a nutty, earthy flavour and a hardy nature that allows them to be rapidly cooked without disintegrating. Tempeh can be found in the refrigerator section of some large supermarkets and health food stores.

Dinner

'Shroom congee

SHIITAKE MUSHROOMS ARE NO SLOUCH IN THE NUTRITION DEPARTMENT, OFFERING ANTIVIRAL, ANTIFUNGAL AND ANTIBACTERIAL PROPERTIES.

- **2 cups (500ml) peanut oil**
- **200g (6½ ounces) shiitake mushrooms, stalks removed, 4 whole and remainder sliced**
- **12cm (4¾-inch) piece fresh ginger, sliced thinly**
- **1 cup (215g) sushi rice**
- **2 litres (8 cups) salt-reduced vegetable stock**
- **2 cups (500ml) water**
- **200g (6½ ounces) enoki mushrooms, stalks trimmed**
- **6 shallots (150g), sliced thinly**
- **6 large cloves garlic, sliced thinly**
- **2 green onions (scallions), sliced thinly**
- **½ cup loosely packed fresh coriander (cilantro) leaves**
- **¼ cup (70g) thai chilli jam paste**
- **¼ cup (60ml) water, extra**
- **2 teaspoons tamari**
- **2 teaspoons sesame oil**

1 Heat 2 tablespoons of the peanut oil in a large wok over high heat; stir-fry whole shiitakes for 4 minutes or until tender; set aside. Stir-fry sliced shiitake mushrooms and ginger for 4 minutes. Add rice; stir-fry for a further 2 minutes. Add stock and the water; cover wok, bring to the boil. Uncover; reduce heat. Simmer, uncovered, for 40 minutes or until congee is thick like porridge, stirring frequently to avoid the base catching. Skim any foam from the top with a spoon during cooking and discard.

2 Meanwhile, heat remaining oil in a small saucepan to 180°C/350°F. Fry enoki for 40 seconds or until golden and crisp; remove from pan with a slotted spoon, drain on paper towel. Fry shallots for 2 minutes or until golden and crisp; remove from pan with slotted spoon, drain on paper towel. Fry garlic for 30 seconds or until just golden; remove from pan with slotted spoon, drain on paper towel. Be careful not to cook garlic too long or it will be bitter. Gently toss cooled enoki, shallot and garlic with green onion and coriander in a small bowl.

3 Combine chilli jam with the extra water in a small bowl.

4 Serve congee drizzled with chilli jam, tamari and sesame oil. Top with whole shiitake mushrooms and fried enoki mixture. Serve immediately.

TIPS You can buy fried shallots and garlic from Asian grocers to save time. Substitute swiss brown mushrooms for shiitakes, if you prefer. If you have left over congee, keep refrigerated in an airtight container, separate from the garnishes, for up to 2 days. Reheat with some hot water to adjust the consistency. SERVING IDEAS Serve topped with chopped roasted peanuts or cashews for extra protein.

Smoky chilli agadashi tofu

FOR A MILDER BROTH, REMOVE THE SEEDS AND MEMBRANES FROM THE CHILLIES, OR USE ONE CHILLI.

- **2 fresh long red chillies**
- **3 teaspoons black rice (see tips)**
- **3 cups (750ml) salt-reduced vegetable stock**
- **1 cinnamon stick**
- **2 star anise**
- **1½ tablespoons tamari**
- **1 strip orange rind**
- **1 litre (4 cups) rice bran oil**
- **2 x 300g (9½-ounce) blocks extra soft silken tofu**
- **1 cup (180g) rice flour**
- **1 green onion (scallion), sliced thinly**
- **8 sprigs fresh coriander (cilantro)**

1 Heat a flat grill plate (or barbecue plate) over medium-high heat. Grill chillies for 3½ minutes on each side, covered with an upturned baking dish to keep the smoke in. Cool; slice thinly.

2 Meanwhile, place rice on grill plate; cook, stirring, for 50 seconds or until rice is cracked. Pound rice with a mortar and pestle until fine (or process in a small food processor).

3 Place stock in a medium saucepan with cinnamon, star anise, tamari and rind. Bring to the boil over high heat; reduce heat to a simmer. Simmer, uncovered, for 5 minutes.

4 Heat oil in a deep medium frying pan over high heat until hot. Drain tofu; pat dry. Cut each block of tofu into six cubes. Toss tofu in flour; shake off excess flour. Season tofu. Use a slotted spoon to lower tofu into oil; fry tofu, in batches, for 1 minute or until golden. Remove from pan with slotted spoon; drain on paper towel.

5 Divide broth among four bowls, place fried tofu in the centre carefully as it will be soft. Top with rice, chilli, green onion and coriander. Serve immediately.

TIPS You can use any rice for this recipe. Gluten-free soy sauce can replace tamari. Make extra stock and keep in the freezer as an Asian master stock for braising vegetables.

PREP + COOK TIME 2 HOURS 30 MINUTES
MAKES 2.5 LITRES (10 CUPS)

Basic stocks

STOCKS ARE EASY TO PREPARE
AND WILL BOOST THE FLAVOUR
OF ANY DISH. THE KEY TO
LOCKING IN THE FLAVOUR IS
TO COOK THEM AT A GENTLE
SIMMER, RATHER THAN AT A BOIL.
FREEZE ANY LEFTOVER STOCK IN
ICE CUBE TRAYS FOR LATER USE.

everyday vegetable stock Coarsely chop 1 medium
(350g) leek, 1 large (200g) unpeeled onion, 2 large (360g)
carrots, 1 large (400g) swede, 2 celery stalks (with leaves)
(300g) and 3 unpeeled garlic cloves. Place vegetables in
a boiler with 1 teaspoon black peppercorns, 2 bay leaves,
2 sprigs each fresh rosemary, thyme and flat-leaf parsley.
and 5 litres (20 cups) water; bring to the boil. Reduce
heat; simmer, for 2 hours. Strain stock through a sieve
into a large bowl; discard solids. Allow stock to cool.
Cover; refrigerate until cold.

italian-flavour stock Coarsely chop 2 large (400g)
unpeeled onions, 2 large (360g) carrots, 2 celery stalks
(with leaves) (300g) and 3 unpeeled cloves garlic.
Place ingredients in a boiler with 1 teaspoon black
peppercorns, 2 bay leaves, 2 sprigs each fresh rosemary
and thyme, 1 teaspoon fennel seeds, 400g (12½ ounces)
canned whole peeled tomatoes and 5 litres (20 cups)
water. Cook following the directions for everyday
vegetable stock above.

asian-flavour stock Coarsely chop 1 medium (350g) leek,
2 large (360g) carrots, 2 celery stalks (with leaves) (300g),
3 unpeeled cloves garlic, 10cm (4-inch) piece ginger and
4 green onions (scallions). Place ingredients in a boiler
with 1 teaspoon black peppercorns, 20 sprigs fresh
coriander (cilantro), 1 cinnamon stick, 3 star anise, ½ cup
(125ml) tamari and 5 litres (20 cups) water. Cook following
the directions for everyday vegetable stock above.

Grilled vegetables with sundried tomato cream

SUNDRIED TOMATOES ARE A FAVOURITE IN THE VEGAN KITCHEN FOR THEIR MOREISH QUALITIES WHICH ARE DUE TO THEIR NATURALLY OCCURRING GLUTAMATES.

You will need to start this recipe at least 4 hours ahead.

- 400g (14 ounces) large heirloom tomatoes, sliced thickly crossways
- olive-oil spray
- 8 baby zucchini with flowers (150g), halved lengthways
- 12 baby eggplant (720g), halved lengthways
- ½ cup firmly packed fresh small basil leaves
- ½ cup micro herbs

SUNDRIED TOMATO CREAM
- 1 cup (140g) raw macadamias
- ¾ cup (110g) drained sundried tomatoes in oil
- 2 tablespoons lemon juice
- 1 small clove garlic, peeled
- 2 tablespoons olive oil
- ¾ cup (180ml) water

1 Make sundried tomato cream.

2 Preheat grill plate (or barbecue) on medium-high. Coat tomato with oil spray; season. Cook tomato for 1 minute each side or until softened. Transfer to a tray; cover to keep warm.

3 Coat zucchini with oil spray; season. Cook zucchini for 2 minutes each side or until grill marks appear and it is just tender. Transfer to tray with tomatoes; cover to keep warm.

4 Coat eggplant with oil spray; season. Grill for 3 minutes each side or until tender. Transfer to tray with vegetables; cover to keep warm.

5 To assemble, spread ½ cup of the sundried tomato cream on a platter. Top with grilled vegetables, remaining sundried tomato cream, basil and micro herbs. Season.

sundried tomato cream Place macadamias in a small bowl; cover with filtered water. Stand for 4 hours; drain. Blend in a high-powered blender with sundried tomatoes, juice, garlic, oil and the water until smooth. Season to taste.

TIPS Sundried tomato cream will keep in the fridge for up to one week. Use as a dip with vegetable sticks or smear on crackers or in a sandwich.
SWAP Use regular eggplant if baby eggplant is unavailable. Use all red tomatoes in place of a mixture of red and green. Cashews, almonds and brazil nuts can be used instead of macadamias.
SERVING IDEA Add grilled slices of tofu to make a main course.

Freekeh tabbouleh with pea felafel

YOU CAN ALSO SERVE THE FELAFEL WITH ONE OF THE BASIC DRESSINGS (PAGE 80) OR BASIC SAUCES (PAGE 140).

You will need to start this recipe the day before.

- ⅔ cup (150g) cracked freekeh
- 1 medium red onion (170g), chopped finely
- 200g (6½ ounces) grape tomatoes, sliced thinly
- 4 cups loosely packed fresh flat-leaf parsley leaves, chopped finely
- 4 cups loosely packed fresh mint leaves, chopped finely
- ¼ cup (60ml) red wine vinegar
- 2 tablespoons olive oil
- ¾ cup (210g) vegan yoghurt (see page 40)
- 2 tablespoons fresh mint leaves, extra

FELAFEL

- 1½ cups (300g) yellow split peas
- 1 tablespoon ground cumin
- 1 tablespoon ground coriander
- 1 small onion (80g), chopped coarsely
- 1 cup loosely packed fresh mint leaves
- 1 cup loosely packed fresh coriander (cilantro) leaves
- ¼ cup (35g) chickpea flour (besan)
- 1 tablespoon water
- rice bran oil, for shallow-frying

1 Make felafel.
2 Cook freekeh in a medium saucepan of boiling salted water for 12 minutes or until tender; drain. Spread freekeh over a large tray; cool.
3 Place freekeh in a large bowl with onion, tomato and herbs. Add combined vinegar and oil; toss well. Season.
4 Serve tabbouleh and felafel topped with yoghurt and extra mint.

felafel Place peas in a medium bowl; cover with filtered water. Stand overnight; drain. Rinse peas; drain well. Process peas with remaining ingredients, except oil, until mixture forms a paste. Season to taste. Using two dessert spoons, shape heaped spoonfuls of pea mixture into ovals (quenelles). Place ovals on an oiled oven tray. Heat rice bran oil in a medium frying pan to 160°C/325°F. Shallow-fry felafel for 2 minutes, in batches, until browned all over and cooked through. Remove from pan with slotted spoon; drain on paper towel. Cover to keep warm.

TIP You can also roll the felafel mixture into balls.
DO AHEAD Felafel can prepared a day ahead and refrigerated. Fry close to serving.

Italian 'cheesy' moxballs

THE MOXBALLS ARE MADE HEARTY WITH PSYLLIUM HUSKS, A WATER SOLUBLE FIBRE THAT WILL FILL YOU UP AND HELP THE BODY WITH ITS NATURAL TOXIN REMOVAL PROCESS.

You will need to make moxarella on page 158 for this recipe.

- **700g (1½ pounds) bottled passata (pureed sieved tomato)**
- **⅔ cup (240g) moxarella (see page 158)**
- **¼ cup loosely packed fresh oregano leaves**

MOXBALLS

- **1 medium onion (150g), grated coarsely**
- **2 x 297g (9½-ounce) blocks firm tofu**
- **1 clove garlic, crushed**
- **½ teaspoon dried italian seasoning**
- **½ teaspoon ground nutmeg**
- **¼ teaspoon chilli flakes**
- **1 cup (120g) almond meal**
- **¼ cup finely chopped fresh flat-leaf parsley leaves**
- **2 tablespoons psyllium husks**

1 Preheat oven to 220°C/425°F.

2 Make moxballs.

3 Pour half of the passata over base of a lightly oiled 20cm x 30cm (8-inch x 12-inch) shallow baking dish. Top with moxballs and remaining passata. Drop spoonfuls of moxarella evenly over the top.

4 Bake for 20 minutes or until moxballs are heated through. Serve sprinkled with fresh oregano.

moxballs Squeeze excess liquid out of the onion using a clean tea towel; place in a large bowl. Drain tofu; pat dry. Finely crumble tofu into bowl. Add remaining ingredients; season well. Stir until combined. Roll tablespoons of mixture into balls.

SWAP You can use your favourite tomato cooking sauce. Substitute the moxarella for grated vegan cheese, if you like.
SERVING IDEAS Serve moxballs and sauce with egg-free pasta or spaghetti or vegan mashed potatoes. This dish can also be served tapas-style as a starter.

Vegan roast & gravy

THIS IS A VEGAN TAKE ON A TURDUCKEN. TO MAKE THIS A REAL CHRISTMAS FEAST, SERVE WITH PEAS AND ROASTED ORANGE SWEET POTATO.

- ⅔ cup (160ml) water
- ⅓ cup (70g) white quinoa
- 1 extra-large zucchini (350g), halved lengthways
- 1 small leek (200g), white part only
- 1.9kg (3¾-pound) whole butternut pumpkin, halved lengthways
- 1 small onion (80g), chopped
- 2 cloves garlic, peeled
- 2½ tablespoons olive oil
- 2 tablespoons fresh thyme leaves
- 3 teaspoons ground linseed (flax meal)
- 2 tablespoons hot water, extra
- ¼ cup (35g) dried cranberries
- ⅓ cup (35g) hazelnut meal

VEGAN GRAVY

- 50g (1½ ounces) vegan margarine spread
- 1 small onion (80g), chopped finely
- 2 tablespoons plain (all-purpose) or gluten-free flour
- 2 cups (500ml) vegetable stock
- 1 tablespoon tamari

1 Preheat oven to 200°C/400°F.

2 Bring the water to the boil in a small saucepan. Add quinoa; reduce heat. Cook, covered, for 15 minutes or until tender; cool.

3 Scoop flesh from zucchini using a strong spoon, leaving a 5mm (¼-inch) border. Reserve zucchini flesh. Trim leek, if needed, to fit inside zucchini.

4 Scoop seeds from pumpkin; discard. Scoop flesh from pumpkin, making a cavity large enough to fit zucchini. Reserve pumpkin flesh. Trim zucchini, if needed, to fit inside pumpkin.

5 Prick the insides of zucchini and pumpkin with a fork. Process reserved zucchini and pumpkin flesh with onion and garlic until finely chopped.

6 Heat 2 tablespoons of the oil in a large frying pan over medium heat. Add processed vegetables, thyme and quinoa; season. Cook, stirring, for 5 minutes or until tender. Cool.

7 Meanwhile, to make stuffing, combine ground linseed and the extra hot water in a medium bowl; stand for 10 minutes. Combine linseed mixture with quinoa mixture, cranberries and hazelnut meal. Press some of the stuffing into zucchini cavities. Press leek into one half of the zucchini; cover with the other half. Press remaining stuffing into pumpkin cavities. Place stuffed zucchini in one pumpkin half; cover with the other half. Secure pumpkin together with kitchen string. Brush with remaining oil; season. Wrap in foil; place in a roasting pan. Roast for 2 hours or until tender. Stand wrapped for 30 minutes.

8 Make vegan gravy.

9 Remove foil from roast; slice thickly. Serve with gravy.

vegan gravy Heat margarine in a medium saucepan over medium heat. Cook onion, stirring, for 5 minutes or until lightly browned. Add flour; cook, stirring, for 5 minutes or until lightly browned. Gradually stir in stock and tamari. Cook, stirring, for 3 minutes or until thickened. Season to taste.

TIP Buy the leek, zucchini and pumpkin at the same time so you can check if they will fit inside each other.
SERVING IDEAS Serve with cooked peas, seasoned and topped with a little vegan margarine spread, if you like.

Tempeh, mushroom & kale dumplings

YOU CAN FREEZE UNCOOKED DUMPLINGS IN A SINGLE LAYER ON A TRAY. TRANSFER TO AN AIRTIGHT CONTAINER OR SNAP-LOCK BAG AND FREEZE FOR UP TO 3 MONTHS.

- 2 tablespoons olive oil
- 150g (4½ ounces) tempeh, chopped coarsely
- 2 green onions (scallions), half chopped, half julienned
- 150g (4½ ounces) button mushrooms, chopped coarsely
- 50g (1½ ounces) kale, leaves and stems sliced separately
- 2 teaspoons finely grated fresh ginger
- 30 gow gee wrappers (275g)
- 260g (8½ ounces) gai lan (chinese broccoli), cut in half

CHILLI MISO SAUCE
- 2 teaspoons korean hot pepper paste (gochujang) (see tip)
- ½ teaspoon sesame oil
- 1 tablespoon shiro (white) miso
- 1 tablespoon black vinegar
- 2 teaspoons finely grated fresh ginger
- 1 cup (250ml) vegetable stock

1 Heat oil in a large frying pan over high heat. Add tempeh, the chopped green onion, mushroom and kale stems. Cook, stirring, for 5 minutes, or until golden; cool 5 minutes. Place in a bowl of a food processor with kale leaves and ginger; season. Pulse until finely chopped.

2 Divide kale mixture among wrappers; about a heaped teaspoon per wrapper, just off centre. Brush edges lightly with water. Fold wrappers over to completely enclose filling.

3 Place dumplings, in a single layer, in batches, about 2cm (¾-inch) apart, in a baking-paper-lined bamboo steamer. Steam, covered, over wok or a large frying pan of simmering water for about 8 minutes or until dumplings are cooked through. Place gai lan in steamer; steam for 3 minutes or until just tender.

4 Meanwhile, make chilli miso sauce.

5 Serve dumplings and gai lan drizzled with sauce and topped with remaining green onion.

chilli miso sauce Combine all ingredients in a small saucepan; heat until warm.

TIP If you can't find hot pepper paste you can use sambal olek or hot chilli sauce.
SERVING IDEA Scatter with black sesame seeds just before serving.

Basic sauces

EASY TO WHIP UP IN A FLASH, THESE SAUCES CAN TAKE A QUICK AND SIMPLE DINNER TO A NEW LEVEL. SERVE WITH VEGETABLE BURGERS, SALADS, FRITTERS OR ANYTHING THAT NEEDS A BRIGHT FLAVOUR BOOST.

mexican green sauce Seed and coarsely chop 4 fresh long green chillies. Process chillies and ⅓ cup (65g) pepitas (pumpkin seed kernels) until almost combined; the mixture should still have some texture. Transfer to a small bowl; combine with 2 tablespoons lime juice and 100ml olive oil. Season with salt. (Makes ⅔ cup)

raw beetroot hummus Wearing gloves, peel 3 medium beetroot (500g), beetroot; coarsely chop. Process beetroot with ¼ cup (60ml) lemon juice, ½ cup (130g) peanut butter, 1 cup (200g) cannellini beans, 1 teaspoon sea salt flakes, 2 halved cloves garlic, ¼ teaspoon ground cumin and ½ cup fresh coriander leaves until smooth. For a thinner sauce, add olive oil and process until combined. (Makes 2½ cups)

turmeric yoghurt sauce Combine ⅓ cup (90g) hulled tahini, ⅓ cup (80ml) warm water, ¼ cup (60ml) lemon juice, ½ cup vegan coconut yoghurt, a large pinch of sugar and ¼ teaspoon ground turmeric in a small jug or bowl; season to taste. Adjust consistency of sauce with a little more warm water, if needed. (Makes 1½ cups)

Sweet potato 'noodles' with mushroom cashew sauce

TO MAKE THE NOODLES FOR THIS RECIPE YOU WILL NEED A SPIRALISER OR WIDE JULIENNE PEELER, OR YOU CAN IMPROVISE USING A WIDE VEGETABLE PEELER.

You will need to start the recipe the day before.

- **1kg (2 pounds) orange sweet potato, peeled**
- **⅓ cup (80ml) olive oil**
- **⅓ cup fresh sage leaves**
- **250g (8 ounces) swiss brown mushrooms, sliced**
- **200g (6½ ounces) silver beet (swiss chard), leaves and stems sliced thinly separately**
- **1 medium lime (65g), cut into wedges**

CASHEW SAUCE
- **1 cup (150g) raw cashews**
- **2 cloves garlic, crushed**
- **2¼ cups (560ml) water**

1 Make cashew sauce.

2 Spiralise sweet potato following packet instructions to form 'noodles'. Heat 2 tablespoons of the oil in a large frying pan over medium heat. Cook 'noodles', turning occasionally, for 6 minutes or until just tender. Remove from pan; cover to keep warm.

3 Increase heat to high. Heat remaining oil in same pan, add half the sage; cook for 1 minute or until crisp. Remove from pan with a slotted spoon; drain on paper towel. Add remaining sage, mushroom and silver beet stems to pan. Cook, stirring, for 5 minutes or until golden. Add silver beet leaves, cook, stirring, for 2 minutes. Remove from heat; stir in cashew sauce. Season to taste.

4 Serve 'noodles' topped with sauce and fried sage, along with lime wedges.

cashew sauce Place cashews in a large bowl; cover with cold water. Stand, covered, overnight. Drain cashews, rinse under cold water; drain well. Process cashews, garlic and the water until smooth. Mixture will be runny but will thicken when combined with hot ingredients. Season to taste.

SERVING IDEAS You can also serve the sauce with regular spaghetti or konjac vegetable spaghetti. Konjac is a high-fibre vegetable famed for it's capacity to fill with barely any kilojoules.

Mexican slaw with coriander & lime tempeh

TEMPEH IS A PROTEIN-RICH FERMENTED SOY PRODUCT, FROM HEALTH FOOD STORES AND MOST SUPERMARKETS.

- 1 bunch coriander (cilantro)
- ⅓ cup (80ml) lime juice
- ¼ cup (60ml) tamari
- 1 teaspoon coconut sugar
- ¼ teaspoon ground cumin
- pinch cayenne pepper
- 200g (6½-ounce) block tempeh, cut into 5mm (¼-inch) thick slices
- 1 large avocado (320g)
- ½ clove garlic, crushed
- 1 fresh long red chilli, seeded, chopped finely
- 1 medium carrot (120g)
- 1 medium purple carrot (120g)
- 2 cups (160g) finely shredded savoy cabbage
- 4 radishes (140g), trimmed, sliced thinly
- 1 tablespoon olive oil
- 2 tablespoons hulled tahini
- 2 teaspoons pure maple syrup
- 2 teaspoons coconut oil
- 8 soft wholegrain tortillas, warmed

1 Wash coriander well to remove all dirt from stems. Remove leaves from coriander; reserve for slaw. Finely chop roots and stems.

2 Combine 2 tablespoons of the lime juice with tamari, sugar, cumin, cayenne pepper and chopped coriander root and stem in a shallow bowl. Add tempeh; toss to coat well. Cover; refrigerate for at least 2 hours or overnight.

3 To make guacamole, coarsely mash avocado in a small bowl; stir in garlic, chilli and 1 tablespoon of the lime juice. Season to taste; cover tightly.

4 Using a vegetable peeler, peel carrots into long thin ribbons. Combine carrot, cabbage, radish and coriander leaves in a large bowl.

5 Combine olive oil, remaining lime juice, tahini and syrup in a jug or bowl. Add dressing to slaw, toss to combine. Season to taste.

6 Drain tempeh well. Heat coconut oil in a medium frying pan over medium-high heat. Add tempeh; cook for 1 minute each side or until golden.

7 Serve tortillas topped with slaw, tempeh and guacamole. Season to taste.

TIP You can use broad bean (fava bean) or chickpea (garbanzo bean) based tempeh for those avoiding soy products.
SERVING IDEAS You could also serve the tempeh with green goddess tahini yoghurt (see page 140), chilli baconnaise (see page 70) or raw beetroot hummus (see page 140).

Sumac roasted eggplant with orange turmeric yoghurt

YOU CAN USE WHITE, RED, BLACK OR TRI-COLOURED QUINOA FOR THIS RECIPE. WHITE IS THE FASTEST COOKING; RED AND BLACK TAKE A FRACTION LONGER.

- 2 large eggplants (1kg), halved
- ⅓ cup (80ml) olive oil
- 2 teaspoons ground sumac
- 400g (12½ ounces) mixed tomato medley, halved
- 2 teaspoons balsamic vinegar
- 1 cup (200g) white quinoa, rinsed, drained
- 1 litre (4 cups) water
- ½ cup firmly packed fresh mint leaves
- ½ cup (80g) roasted almonds, chopped coarsely
- ½ cup (140g) vegan yoghurt
- 2 tablespoons orange juice
- 1 teaspoon finely grated orange rind
- ½ teaspoon ground turmeric
- 2 tablespoons mint leaves, extra

1 Preheat oven to 200°C/400°F. Line two oven trays with baking paper.

2 Using a small sharp knife, score a criss-cross pattern on cut-side of eggplant halves. Combine 2 tablespoons of the oil and sumac in a small bowl; rub into eggplant, ensuring mixture goes in the cuts. Season well. Place eggplant, cut-side up, on one tray. Roast for 40 minutes or until tender and browned.

3 Meanwhile, toss tomato in 2 teaspoons of the remaining oil and vinegar in a medium bowl; season. Place on remaining oven tray; roast with eggplant for last 15 minutes of eggplant cooking time.

4 Place quinoa and the water in a medium saucepan; bring to the boil. Simmer, uncovered, for 12 minutes or until tender. Drain well; return quinoa to saucepan.

5 Chop mint coarsely. Add chopped mint, tomatoes and almonds to quinoa; toss well. Season to taste. Place quinoa on a platter or plates; drizzle with remaining oil.

6 Combine yoghurt, juice, rind and turmeric in a small bowl; season to taste.

7 Serve quinoa topped with eggplant; drizzle with yoghurt mixture. Sprinkle with extra mint leaves.

SERVING IDEA You can also seve the eggplant with raw beetroot hummus (see page 140).

Lentil bolognese on mung bean fettuccine

MAKE DOUBLE OF THE BOLOGNESE AND FREEZE IT IN INDIVIDUAL PORTIONS FOR UP TO 2 MONTHS.

- 1 tablespoon olive oil
- 1 medium onion (150g), chopped finely
- 3 trimmed stalks celery (300g), chopped finely
- 1 medium carrot (120g), chopped finely
- 200g (6½ ounces) button mushrooms, sliced
- 300g (9½ ounces) pumpkin, grated coarsely
- 2 cloves garlic, crushed
- 2 tablespoons tomato paste
- 2 tablespoons red wine vinegar
- 400g (12½ ounces) canned cherry tomatoes
- 400g (12½ ounces) canned brown lentils, drained, rinsed
- ½ cup firmly packed fresh basil leaves, chopped finely
- 375g (12 ounces) mung bean fettuccine (see tips)
- 1 tablespoon nutritional yeast flakes (see tips)
- 2 tablespoons fresh small basil leaves, extra

1 Heat oil in a large frying pan over medium-high heat. Cook onion, celery and carrot, stirring, for 5 minutes or until soft. Add mushrooms and pumpkin; cook for 3 minutes, stirring occasionally, or until soft. Stir in garlic; cook, stirring, for 1 minute or until fragrant.

2 Stir in paste and vinegar; cook, stirring, for 1 minute. Add tomatoes and lentils; reduce heat to low. Stir in basil. Simmer gently, covered, for 15 minutes. Add a little water if sauce is reducing too quickly. Season to taste.

3 Meanwhile, cook the mung bean fettuccine following packet directions; drain.

4 Serve fettuccine topped with lentil bolognese, sprinkled with yeast flakes and extra basil.

TIPS Nutritional yeast flakes are a complete protein and a good source of B vitamins which makes them great for vegans. They have a complex savoury flavour which makes them a good substitute for parmesan cheese. Mung bean fettuccine is a high-protein alternative to wheat pasta and is suitable for vegans and people who are intolerant to gluten and wheat. It is available from some health food stores.

SWAP You can use your favourite pasta in place of the mung bean fettuccine or rice noodles or steamed spiralised zucchini.

Turmeric coconut crêpes with mixed mushrooms

THE MAIN ACTIVE INGREDIENT IN TURMERIC IS A COMPOUND CALLED CURCUMIN WHICH IN TESTS HAS BEEN SHOWN TO HAVE ANTI-INFLAMMATORY PROPERTIES.

- 1 tablespoon olive oil
- 600g (1¼ pounds) mixed mushrooms, sliced (see tip)
- 2 cloves garlic, crushed
- 6 green onions (scallions), sliced thinly
- 1 tablespoon tamari
- ¾ cup (135g) rice flour
- ¼ teaspoon ground turmeric
- 1 cup (250ml) coconut milk
- ⅓ cup (80ml) cold water
- ½ teaspoon coconut oil
- 1 cup (80g) bean sprouts, trimmed
- 1 cup loosely packed fresh coriander (cilantro) leaves
- 1 cup loosely packed fresh mint leaves
- 2 fresh long red chillies, sliced thinly
- 1 medium lime (90g), cut into wedges

1 Heat the oil in a large frying pan over high heat. Cook mushrooms, in batches, stirring, for 5 minutes or until soft. Add garlic, green onion and tamari, cook, stirring, for 1 minute or until fragrant. Remove from heat; season to taste. Cover to keep warm.

2 Meanwhile, sift flour, turmeric and a pinch of salt into a medium bowl. Make a well in the centre; gradually whisk in combined coconut milk and the water to form a smooth batter.

3 Place a non-stick frying pan (25cm (10-inch) (top measurement), (22cm) (8¾-inch) (base measurement) or crêpe pan over a medium-high heat. Lightly grease with coconut oil. Pour ¼ cup batter into pan, tilting pan to coat the base. Cover pan for 1 minute to steam. Uncover; add a quarter each of the mushroom mixture, sprouts, herbs and chilli. Loosen edge with spatula; fold crêpe then slide out of pan onto a warmed plate. Repeat with remaining batter and ingredients to make four crêpes in total.

4 Serve crêpes with lime wedges.

TIP Choose mostly mild-flavoured mushrooms such as button, swiss browns, oyster and shimeji and use a smaller amount of strong-flavoured shiitake or crunchy enoki.

Rainbow mezze feast

- 2 cups (240g) frozen peas, thawed
- 400g (12½ ounces) canned chickpeas (garbanzo beans), drained, rinsed
- 1 clove garlic, crushed
- ½ cup firmly packed fresh flat-leaf parsley leaves
- ½ cup firmly packed fresh coriander (cilantro) leaves
- 1 teaspoon ground cumin
- 1 teaspoon ground coriander
- 1½ tablespoons plain (all-purpose) flour
- ½ cup (50g) packaged dry breadcrumbs
- 1 teaspoon finely grated lemon rind
- ⅓ cup (80ml) olive oil
- 200g (6 ounces) baby carrots, trimmed

BEETROOT DIP
- 2 medium beetroot (beets) (350g), trimmed
- 2 whole cloves garlic, unpeeled
- 1 cup (100g) walnuts, roasted (see tips)
- 2 tablespoons lemon juice
- 1 tablespoon hulled tahini

CARROT & TURMERIC HUMMUS
- 1 medium carrot (120g), grated coarsely
- 400g (12½ ounces) canned chickpeas (garbanzo beans), drained, rinsed
- 1 tablespoon hulled tahini
- 2 tablespoons lemon juice

- 2 teaspoons freshly grated fresh turmeric (see tips)
- ½ teaspoon ground cumin
- 1 clove garlic, crushed
- ¼ cup (60ml) olive oil

QUINOA TABBOULEH
- ½ cup (100g) white quinoa, rinsed, drained
- 2 cups (500ml) water
- 1 cup firmly packed fresh flat-leaf parsley leaves, chopped finely
- 1 cup firmly packed fresh mint leaves, chopped finely
- 200g (6½ ounces) cherry tomatoes, quartered
- 3 green onions (scallions), sliced thinly
- 1 tablespoon olive oil
- 1 tablespoon lemon juice

1 Make dips and tabbouleh.
2 To make felafel, process peas, chickpeas, garlic, herbs, spices, flour, breadcrumbs and rind until combined; season to taste. Shape 2 tablespoon amounts of mixture into balls; flatten slightly. Place on a plate or tray.
3 Heat oil in a large non-stick frying pan over a medium heat. Cook felafel, in batches, for 2 minutes each side or until golden and heated through.
4 Serve felafel with dips, quinoa tabbouleh and baby carrots.

beetroot dip Preheat oven to 200°C/400°F. Scrub beetroots well. Wrap beetroots individually in foil; place on an oven tray. Roast for 40 minutes. Add whole garlic cloves to tray; roast beetroot and garlic for a further 20 minutes or until tender. Stand beetroot until cool enough to handle. Peel beetroot; chop coarsely. Squeeze flesh from garlic. Process beetroot and garlic with remaining ingredients until smooth. Transfer to a medium bowl; season to taste.

carrot & turmeric hummus Process all ingredients until smooth. Transfer to a medium bowl; season to taste.

quinoa tabbouleh Place quinoa and the water in a medium saucepan; bring to the boil. Reduce heat; simmer, uncovered, for 12 minutes or until tender. Drain well. Transfer quinoa to a medium bowl; combine with herbs, tomato, onion, oil and juice. Season to taste.

TIPS Roasting nuts brings out the flavour. Spread nuts onto an oven tray, roast in a 180°C/350°F oven for 5 to 10 minutes, or until nuts are golden brown (stir nuts once during roasting for even cooking). You can use ¼ teaspoon ground turmeric if fresh is unavailable.

DO-AHEAD Dips and tabbouleh can be made and felafel prepared to the end of step 2 several hours ahead; cover and keep refrigerated. Stand dips at room temperature for 30 minutes before serving and fry felafel just before serving. Felafel can be frozen in a container for up to 1 month.

SERVING IDEAS Serve in a large bowl with lime halves, cucumber ribbons and butter lettuce leaves, if you like.

Thai brussels sprouts curry

USE A MIXTURE OF ASIAN MUSHROOMS SUCH AS OYSTER, SHIMEJI AND STRAW MUSHROOMS.

- 2 cups (500ml) coconut milk
- 1½ cups (375ml) vegetable stock
- 2 fresh kaffir lime leaves, torn
- 300g (9½ ounces) baby brussels sprouts, halved
- 1 tablespoon lime juice
- 2 teaspoons coconut sugar
- 150g (4½ ounces) green beans, halved diagonally
- 400g (12½ ounces) mixed asian mushrooms
- ⅓ cup fresh thai basil leaves
- ⅓ cup fresh coriander (cilantro) leaves

GREEN CURRY PASTE

- 1 teaspoon ground coriander
- 1 teaspoon ground cumin
- 8 fresh long green chillies, chopped coarsely
- 1 clove garlic, quartered
- 2 green onions (scallions), chopped coarsely
- 10cm (4-inch) stalk lemon grass, white part only, sliced thinly
- 5cm (2-inch) piece fresh ginger, chopped finely
- 1 tablespoon coarsely chopped fresh coriander (cilantro) root and stem mixture
- 2 tablespoons rice bran oil

1 Make green curry paste.

2 Place paste in large saucepan over low-medium heat; cook, stirring for 2 minutes or until fragrant. Add coconut milk, stock and lime leaves; bring to the boil. Reduce heat; simmer, stirring, for 5 minutes.

3 Stir in brussels sprouts, juice and sugar; simmer, covered, for 10 minutes or until sprouts are almost tender. Add beans and mushrooms; cook, covered, stirring occasionally, until vegetables are just tender. Season to taste.

4 Serve curry sprinkled with basil and coriander.

green curry paste Stir coriander and cumin in small frying pan over medium heat until fragrant. Blend or process spices with chilli, garlic, onion, lemon grass, ginger and coriander mixture until mixture forms a coarse paste. Add oil; blend or process until mixture forms a smooth paste. Measure ½ cup of the paste for this recipe, then freeze the remainder (there will be about ½ cup leftover) in a small container for another use.

TIPS Many Thai curry pastes contain shrimp paste or fish sauce so we've made our own. As a short-cut, you can buy a curry paste; check the label carefully. You can remove the seeds from the chillies for a milder paste.

SERVING IDEAS Serve with steamed brown rice, thinly sliced red chilli and fried shallots.

PREP + COOK TIME 15 MINUTES (+ STANDING)
MAKES 3¾ CUPS (900G)

Moxarella

MOXARELLA IS OUR VEGAN
SUBSTITUTE FOR MOZZARELLA.

- ½ cup (75g) raw cashews
- ½ cup (70g) macadamias
- 3 cups (750ml) filtered water
- ⅔ cup (100g) arrowroot
- ¼ cup (60ml) avocado oil (see tips)
- ¼ cup (25g) nutritional yeast flakes
  (see Vegan Pantry, page 9)
- 2 teaspoons sea salt flakes
- 2 tablespoons lemon juice

1 Place cashews in a small bowl; cover with cold water.
Stand, covered, for 4 hours or overnight. Drain cashews,
rinse under cold water; drain well. Add cashews to a
high-powered blender with remaining ingredients;
blend until smooth.
2 Pour mixture into a medium saucepan. Cook, stirring,
over a medium heat for 9 minutes or until mixture becomes
very thick and stretchy like melted pizza cheese.
3 Pour mixture into a 3 cup (750ml) container; cool.
Cover with the lid; refrigerate.

DO-AHEAD Moxarella will keep in a covered container in
the fridge for up to 1 week.

chilli & garlic moxarella Finely chop two small seeded
fresh red chillies and two cloves of garlic. Pour 1 quantity
moxarella into a medium bowl, fold in chilli and garlic.

olive & rosemary moxarella Remove seeds from 60g
(2oz) sicilian olives; chop coarsely. Chop 1 tablespoon
fresh rosemary leaves. Pour 1 quantity moxarella into a
medium bowl, fold in olives and rosemary.

TIPS Use moxarella as a cheese
substitute on pizza, toasted sandwiches,
oven bakes or as a savoury spread on
crackers. Use olive oil or grapeseed oil
in place of avocado oil or try adding a
punch with chilli oil.

Beet bourguignon

BEETS REPLACE BEEF IN THIS TWIST ON THE FRENCH CLASSIC, BEEF BOURGUIGNON. INSTEAD OF THE TRADITIONAL GARNISH OF BACON TRY CRISP TEMPEH.

- ¼ cup (60ml) olive oil
- 8 shallots (200g), halved (see tip)
- 500g (1 pound) baby beetroot (beets), quartered
- 2 medium carrots (240g), chopped coarsely
- 200g (6½ ounces) button mushrooms, halved or quartered
- 200g (6½ ounces) swiss brown mushrooms, halved
- 3 cloves garlic, chopped finely
- 2 fresh bay leaves
- 2 sprigs fresh rosemary
- 2 sprigs fresh thyme
- 2 tablespoons plain (all-purpose) flour
- 2 tablespoons tomato paste
- 1 cup (250ml) vegan dry red wine
- 2 cups (500ml) vegetable stock
- 2 cups (500ml) water
- 400g (12½ ounces) canned borlotti beans, drained, rinsed
- 2 tablespoons micro herbs

1 Heat oil in a large saucepan over medium heat. Cook shallots, stirring, for 10 minutes or until softened. Add beetroot, carrot, mushrooms, garlic, bay leaves, rosemary and thyme; cook, stirring, for 5 minutes or until golden.

2 Add flour; cook, stirring; for 2 minutes. Stir in paste; cook for 1 minute.

3 Gradually stir in wine; cook, stirring, for 1 minute. Add stock and the water; simmer, partially covered, for 40 minutes or until beetroot is almost tender.

4 Add beans; cook for 5 minutes or until heated through. Discard bay leaves, rosemary and thyme sprigs.

5 Serve sprinkled with micro herbs.

TIP Shallots are also known as eschallots or French shallots.

SERVING IDEAS Serve with mashed potato prepared with vegan milk and olive oil.

Beer battered tofu & seasoned wedges

WASH AND DRY THE SWEET POTATO. CUT INTO WEDGES WITH THE SKIN ON FOR EXTRA FLAVOUR AND NUTRIENTS.

- 2 x 300g (9½ ounces) packets firm tofu
- 1 tablespoon finely grated lemon rind
- ⅓ cup (80ml) lemon juice
- 2 cloves garlic, crushed
- 1 teaspoon cracked black pepper
- ⅔ cup (100g) plain (all-purpose) spelt flour
- ¼ cup (35g) cornflour (cornstarch)
- ¼ cup (40g) instant polenta (cornmeal)
- 1 teaspoon baking powder
- ¼ teaspoon sea salt flakes
- ¼ teaspoon garlic powder
- ¼ teaspoon onion powder
- 1½ cups (375ml) vegan beer
- 1kg (2 pounds) orange sweet potato, cut into thin wedges
- 2 tablespoons rice bran oil
- rice bran oil, for shallow-frying, extra
- ⅔ cup (100g) cornflour (cornstarch), extra
- 1 medium lemon (140g), cut into wedges

SPICE MIX
- 1 tablespoon celery salt
- ½ teaspoon mild paprika
- large pinch freshly ground black pepper
- large pinch cayenne pepper

1 Drain tofu; pat dry. Cut each block of tofu lengthways into four thick slices. Combine rind, juice, garlic and pepper in a shallow glass or ceramic dish. Add tofu; turn to coat. Cover; refrigerate for 3 hours, turning occasionally.

2 Combine flours, polenta, baking powder, salt, garlic and onion powders in a medium bowl. Gradually whisk in beer until the consistency of pancake batter. Cover; refrigerate for 1 hour.

3 Meanwhile, preheat oven to 220°C/425°F. Line an oven tray with baking paper.

4 Place sweet potato on tray; drizzle with oil, season. Toss to coat. Roast for 45 minutes or until tender.

5 Make spice mix.

6 Heat the extra oil in a large saucepan over medium-high heat. Dust tofu in extra cornflour, shake away excess. Dip tofu in batter; drain away excess. Shallow-fry tofu, in batches, for 1 minute each side or until golden on both sides and heated through. Drain on paper towel.

7 Sprinkle tofu and sweet potato wedges with spice mix and serve with lemon wedges. Season to taste.

spice mix Combine ingredients in a small bowl.

TIP You can use soda water instead of beer.
SERVING IDEAS Serve with vegan tartare sauce or chilli baconaise (see page 70).

Vegetable gado gado with peanut sauce

THE PEANUT SAUCE CAN BE MADE SEVERAL HOURS AHEAD AND THE VEGETABLES CAN BE CUT, READY TO GO, HOWEVER, STEAM THEM JUST BEFORE EATING.

- 2 corn cobs (800g), husk and silk removed
- ½ small green cabbage (600g), cut into wedges
- 2 small orange sweet potato (270g), sliced thickly
- 1 large zucchini (150g), sliced thickly
- 1 medium red capsicum (bell pepper) (200g), sliced thickly
- 200g (6½ ounces) sugar snap peas, trimmed
- 1 cup (80g) bean sprouts
- 2 fresh long red chillies, seeded, cut into thin strips
- ¼ cup (20g) shredded coconut, toasted
- ¼ cup (35g) coarsely chopped roasted peanuts
- 2 tablespoons white sesame seeds, toasted
- 2 tablespoons fried asian shallots
- ½ cup loosely packed fresh coriander (cilantro) sprigs

PEANUT SAUCE
- 1 cup (280g) crunchy peanut butter
- 1 cup (250ml) canned coconut milk
- 1 fresh kaffir lime leaf, shredded
- 2 teaspoons sesame oil
- 2 tablespoons tamari
- ¼ cup (60ml) lime juice

1 Line two large steamer baskets with baking paper; pierce holes in paper.
2 Place one steamer over a wok of simmering water. Cut corn into quarters. Place corn, cabbage and sweet potato in basket; cover with lid, steam for 5 minutes. Remove lid, add zucchini and capsicum to second steamer; place on top of steamer in wok. Cover top steamer with lid, steam for 5 minutes or until vegetables are almost tender. Add peas to top steamer; cover, steam for 2 minutes or until vegetables are just tender.

3 Meanwhile, make peanut sauce.
4 Spread peanut sauce on a platter, top with steamed vegetable, then sprinkle with sprouts, chilli, coconut, peanuts, seeds, shallots and coriander.
peanut sauce Whisk all ingredients in a medium bowl until combined; season to taste.

TIPS You can use your favourite vegetables in this versatile Indonesian salad – steamed green beans, potato and broccoli and raw vegetables, such as cucumber and tomatoes. Add tofu or tempeh for a more substantial meal.

Roast chilli jam vegetables with thai cucumber salad

THE BEST WAY TO STORE THAI BASIL IS OUT OF THE FRIDGE OR IT WILL SHRIVEL AND BLACKEN. PLACE THE BUNCH IN A JUG OF WATER, COVERED WITH A PLASTIC BAG.

- ½ cup (150g) thai chilli jam paste
- ¼ cup (50g) coconut oil, melted
- 800g (1½ pounds) kent pumpkin, cut into wedges
- 400g (12½ ounces) baby carrots, trimmed
- 2 lebanese cucumbers (260g), seeded, sliced on the diagonal
- 2 green onions (scallions), sliced thinly
- 2 cups (160g) bean sprouts
- ½ cup loosely packed fresh thai basil leaves
- ½ cup loosely packed fresh round mint leaves
- 1 fresh long red chilli, sliced thinly
- ¼ cup (60ml) lime juice
- 2 tablespoons brown sugar
- 1 teaspoon sesame oil
- 1 tablespoon coarsely chopped salted peanuts

1 Preheat oven to 180°C/350°F. Line two oven trays with baking paper.
2 Combine chilli jam and coconut oil in a small bowl. Rub over pumpkin and carrots; place on trays. Roast vegetables for 30 minutes or until just tender.
3 Meanwhile, combine cucumber, green onion, sprouts, herbs and chilli in a medium bowl.
4 To make dressing, place juice, sugar and sesame oil in a screw-top jar, shake well. Season to taste. Pour over cucumber mixture; toss to combine.
5 Serve roast vegetables topped with cucumber salad and peanuts.

DO-AHEAD Dressing can be made 2 days ahead; keep refrigerated in a screw-top jar. SERVING IDEA Serve with steamed jasmine or brown rice.

Hoisin-baked eggplant with steamed greens

USE YOUR FAVOURITE GREENS IN THIS RECIPE; BROCCOLI, CHOY SUM, GAI LAN, ASPARAGUS AND GREEN OR SNAKE BEANS WOULD ALL WORK WELL.

- **2 medium eggplants (600g), sliced thickly**
- **1 cup (280g) hoisin sauce**
- **1 tablespoon sesame seeds**
- **2 teaspoons black sesame seeds**
- **270g (8½ ounces) buckwheat soba noodles**
- **½ cup (125ml) tamari**
- **2 tablespoons brown sugar**
- **1 tablespoon sesame oil**
- **175g (5½ ounces) broccolini**
- **1 baby buk choy (50g)**

1 Preheat oven to 180°C/350°F. Line two oven trays with baking paper.

2 Place eggplant on trays in a single layer; brush both sides with sauce. Sprinkle with seeds. Bake eggplant for 20 minutes or until tender.

3 Meanwhile, cook noodles in a large saucepan of boiling salted water for 3 minutes or until just tender. Drain; cover to keep warm.

4 To make dressing, whisk tamari, sugar and oil in a small bowl. Place noodles and half the dressing in a large bowl; toss to combine.

5 Boil, steam or microwave broccolini and buk choy until tender; drain.

6 Serve eggplant with noodles, greens and remaining dressing. Top with thinly sliced green onion, if you like.

TIP Take care not to overcook the noodles as they will continue to cook once drained.

Shepherdless pie

WHO NEEDS LAMB WHEN YOU HAVE LENTILS, MUSHROOMS, A RAINBOW OF OTHER TASTY VEGETABLES AND A PILLOWY POLENTA CRUST?

- 1 cup (200g) french-style green lentils
- 2 tablespoons olive oil
- 1 medium onion (150g), chopped coarsely
- 2 cloves garlic, crushed
- 2 teaspoons fennel seeds
- 1 medium carrot (120g), chopped coarsely
- 200g (6½ ounces) swiss brown mushrooms, halved
- 400g (12½ ounces) grape tomatoes
- 2 tablespoons tomato paste
- 1 cup (250ml) vegetable stock
- 60g (2 ounces) baby spinach
- fresh thyme leaves, extra, to serve

POLENTA TOPPING
- 1 litre (4 cups) vegetable stock
- 1 cup (170g) polenta (cornmeal)
- 2 tablespoons finely chopped fresh thyme leaves
- 2 tablespoons olive oil
- 2 tablespoons nutritional yeast flakes (see Vegan Pantry, page 9)

1 Cook lentils in a medium saucepan of boiling water, uncovered, for 12 minutes or until just tender; drain.

2 Meanwhile, heat oil in a large deep frying pan over medium-high heat. Cook onion, garlic and seeds, stirring, for 5 minutes or until onion is soft. Add carrot, mushrooms and tomatoes; cook covered, for 10 minutes, or until carrot softens. Stir in paste; cook for 1 minute. Add in stock; bring to the boil. Cook, uncovered, for 3 minutes or until thickened slightly. Stir in lentils and spinach; season to taste. Cover to keep warm.

3 Make polenta topping.

4 Preheat grill (broiler) on high. Place lentil mixture in a 2-litre (8-cup) ovenproof dish; spread with polenta topping. Grill for 15 minutes or until golden and crisp.

5 Serve topped with extra thyme. Season to taste.

polenta topping Bring stock to the boil in a large saucepan. Gradually add polenta and thyme to stock, stirring constantly. Reduce heat; cook, stirring, for 10 minutes or until polenta thickens. Stir in oil and yeast. Season to taste.

TIP French-style green lentils, grown in Australia, are related to the famous French lentils du puy; these green-blue, tiny lentils have a nutty, earthy flavour and a hardy nature that allows them to be rapidly cooked without disintegrating.

Nuts & sprouts pilaf

CRUNCHY COMBO SPROUTS ARE A MIX OF BLUE PEA, RED COOLONA, MUNG BEAN AND LENTIL SPROUTS. ALTERNATIVELY CREATE YOUR OWN SPROUT MIX.

- 500g (1 pound) butternut pumpkin, unpeeled, cut into 1.5cm (¾-inch) thick half-moon slices
- 2½ tablespoons olive oil
- 1 large onion (300g), chopped finely
- 3 cloves garlic, crushed
- ¼ cup (40g) coarsely chopped natural almonds
- ¼ cup (40g) coarsely chopped brazil nuts
- 2 teaspoons baharat (see tips)
- 1½ cups (300g) brown rice
- 1 litre (4 cups) vegetable stock
- ¼ cup (50g) pepitas (pumpkin seed kernels)
- 200g (6½ ounces) crunchy combo sprouts (see note above)
- ½ cup loosely packed fresh dill sprigs
- ½ cup loosely packed fresh flat-leaf parsley leaves
- ¾ cup (200g) coconut or vegan yoghurt

1 Preheat oven to 200°C/400°F. Line an oven tray with baking paper.

2 Combine pumpkin and 2 teaspoons of the oil on tray. Roast for 30 minutes or until golden and tender.

3 Meanwhile, heat remaining oil in a large saucepan over medium heat. Cook onion, garlic and nuts, stirring occasionally, for 7 minutes or until onion is soft. Add baharat; cook, stirring, for 1 minute or until fragrant.

4 Add rice to pan; cook, stirring, for 2 minutes or until rice is coated. Add stock, bring to the boil; reduce heat to low. Cook, covered, for 35 minutes. Cook, uncovered, for further 10 minutes or until liquid is absorbed and rice is tender. Remove from heat; stir in pepitas, half the sprouts and half the herbs. Stand covered, for 10 minutes. Season to taste.

5 Place pumpkin on a platter. Top with pilaf, remaining sprouts and herbs, and yoghurt. Season. Serve with lemon wedges, if you like.

TIPS Baharat is a Middle Eastern spice mix found in delis, gourmet food stores or Middle Eastern grocers. Baharat can vary in flavour and strength between brands, we suggest adjusting to taste. If unavailable, you can substitute ras el hanout or a Moroccan spice blend.

Sweet potato & 'chorizo' Tacos

OUR PIQUANT SUNDRIED TOMATO TACO FILLING IS INSPIRED BY THE BOLD SPICINESS OF CHORIZO SAUSAGE.

- **2 small orange sweet potato (500g), unpeeled**
- **½ cup (125ml) olive oil**
- **6 green onions (scallions), chopped coarsely**
- **1 teaspoon ground cumin**
- **1 teaspoon ground coriander**
- **2 cups coarsely chopped fresh coriander (cilantro) roots and stems**
- **2 fresh jalapeño chillies, chopped coarsely**
- **1½ teaspoons finely grated lime rind**
- **2 tablespoons lime juice**
- **⅓ cup (80ml) water**
- **500g (1 pound) bottled sundried tomatoes in oil**
- **¼ teaspoon garlic powder**
- **¼ teaspoon onion powder**
- **½ teaspoon smoked paprika**
- **¼ cup (40g) roasted whole blanched almonds**
- **¼ cup (25g) roasted walnuts**
- **12 x 17cm (6¾-inch) white corn tortillas, warmed**
- **40g (1½ ounces) baby rocket (arugula) leaves**

1 Boil, steam or microwave sweet potato until tender; drain. When cool enough to handle, peel sweet potato; cut flesh into 1.5cm (¾-inch) pieces.

2 Meanwhile, blend or process oil, green onion, cumin, ground coriander, fresh coriander, chillies, rind, juice and the water until smooth. Transfer to a small bowl; stand until required.

3 Drain oil from tomatoes over a bowl; reserve. Coarsely chop tomatoes. Process tomatoes and 2 tablespoons of the reserved oil with garlic and onion powders, paprika and nuts until coarsely chopped. Add 2 tablespoons of coriander mixture; pulse until combined.

4 Transfer tomato mixture to a large frying pan, stir in sweet potato. Heat mixture over low heat for 5 minutes or until warmed through.

5 Serve tortillas filled with sweet potato mixture and rocket, topped with remaining coriander mixture.

SERVING IDEAS Accompany with vegan green goddess tahini yoghurt (see page 80) or avocado mashed with lemon juice. Serve with lime halves, fresh coriander leaves, thinly sliced green onion and sriracha chilli sauce, if you like.

Zucchini & Tofu noodles with coriander pesto

YELLOW PATTY PAN SQUASH, ALSO KNOWN AS BUTTON SQUASH, ARE A SUMMER VEGETABLE; IF UNAVAILABLE SUBSTITUTE WITH YELLOW OR GREY ZUCCHINI.

- ¼ cup (60ml) olive oil
- 500g (16 ounces) firm tofu, cubed
- 250g (8 ounces) yellow patty pan squash, halved crossways
- 350g (11 ounces) zucchini, halved lengthways, chopped coarsely
- 2 teaspoons finely grated fresh ginger
- 2 cloves garlic, crushed
- 1 tablespoon light soy sauce
- 180g (5½ ounces) dried soba noodles
- ½ cup (75g) roasted cashews, chopped coarsely
- 1 cup loosely packed fresh coriander (cilantro) leaves

CORIANDER PESTO

- 1 cup (150g) roasted cashews
- 3 cups loosely packed fresh coriander (cilantro) leaves
- 1 clove garlic, crushed
- 2 teaspoons finely grated lemon rind
- 1 tablespoon lemon juice
- 1 fresh long green chilli, seeded, chopped coarsely
- ½ cup (125ml) olive oil

1 Make coriander pesto.

2 Heat 2 tablespoons of the oil in a large deep frying pan over high heat; cook tofu for 3 minutes each side or until golden. Remove from pan; cover to keep warm.

3 Heat remaining oil in same pan; cook squash and zucchini, stirring, for 5 minutes or until golden and tender. Add ginger and garlic; cook, stirring for 30 seconds or until fragrant. Add sauce; cook for 1 minute.

4 Meanwhile, cook noodles in a large saucepan of boiling water, uncovered, until just tender; drain. Return noodles to pan, add pesto; toss to combine.

5 Serve noodles with zucchini mixture and tofu; top with cashews and coriander.

coriander pesto Blend or process ingredients until smooth; season to taste.

TIP You will need to buy 3 bunches of coriander (cilantro) for this recipe.

Sweets

Hibiscus creams

FINDING A VEGAN WHITE CHOCOLATE ISN'T EASY, AS MILK PRODUCTS ARE A MAJOR COMPONENT, BUT THE GOOD NEWS IS YOU CAN MAKE YOUR OWN WITH OUR RECIPE.

- ½ cup (75g) raw cashews
- 1 tablespoon hibiscus loose-leaf tea
- ¼ cup (60ml) boiling water
- 1 cup (120g) frozen raspberries, thawed
- ¼ cup (50g) coconut oil, melted
- ¼ cup (60g) cacao butter, melted
- ¼ cup (60ml) coconut cream
- 2 tablespoons coconut nectar
- ½ teaspoon pure vanilla extract

WHITE CHOCOLATE
- ½ cup (120g) cacao butter, melted
- ⅓ cup (80g) coconut butter or paste (see tips)
- ¼ cup (70g) cashew butter
- 2 tablespoons coconut nectar
- ½ teaspoon pure vanilla extract
- 1½ teaspoons soy milk powder, optional (see tips)

1 Place cashews in a small bowl; cover with cold water. Stand, covered, for 4 hours or overnight. Drain cashews, rinse under cold water; drain well.

2 Place tea in a cup; cover with the boiling water. Stand tea for 4 to 6 hours; strain into a cup or jug. Discard leaves.

3 Blend or process tea with drained cashews, raspberries with any juice, coconut oil, cacao butter, coconut cream, nectar and vanilla until as smooth as possible (see tips).

4 Pour mixture into an ice cube tray or silicon moulds (see tips); tap gently on bench to level. Freeze for 5 hours or until firm.

5 Remove hibiscus creams from ice cube tray; place on a tray lined with baking paper. Return to freezer while preparing white chocolate.

6 Make white chocolate. Using a fork, lower hibiscus creams, one at a time, into chocolate to coat. Allow excess chocolate to drain off, then place on tray. Freeze for 5 minutes or until chocolate is firm. Keep leftover chocolate warm, over hot water. Repeat dipping to double-coat hibiscus creams; freeze for 10 minutes or until chocolate is firm.

white chocolate Combine cacao butter, coconut butter and cashew butter in a medium heatproof bowl over a bowl of hot water until as smooth as possible. Add nectar, vanilla and soy milk powder; stir until combined. Pour into a small bowl.

TIPS Use a good-quality coconut butter that is creamy and not too dry. To melt coconut butter, place jar in a small bowl of boiling water; stand for 5 minutes, then stir to combine.

Soy milk powder is available from most health food stores. It makes the white chocolate extra creamy, however it will still work without it.

Use heart-shaped silicone moulds for Valentine's Day chocolates.

If you have one, use a high-powered blender in step 3; this type of blender will produce a very smooth consistency.

DO-AHEAD Store in an airtight container in the fridge for up to 5 days. Creams can be frozen in a container for up to 2 months. Creams are best eaten within 30 minutes of removing from freezer.

Ginger, coconut & almond slice

THE SLICE KEEPS WELL IN AN AIRTIGHT CONTAINER IN THE FRIDGE FOR UP TO 1 WEEK, OR CAN BE FROZEN FOR UP TO 2 MONTHS; THAW IN THE FRIDGE.

You will need to start this recipe the day before.

- 1½ cups (225g) cashews
- 1 young drinking coconut (1.2kg)
- 1½ cups (240g) natural almonds
- 1 cup (140g) pitted dried dates, chopped coarsely
- ½ cup (40g) shredded coconut
- ¾ cup (165g) crystallised ginger, sliced thinly
- ¾ cup (180ml) melted coconut oil
- ½ cup (125ml) rice malt syrup
- 2 tablespoons finely grated fresh ginger
- ½ cup (125ml) coconut milk
- 1½ teaspoons vanilla extract
- 2 tablespoons flaked almonds, roasted, to serve

1 Place cashews in a medium bowl; cover with cold water. Stand, covered, for 1 hour. Drain cashews, rinse under cold water; drain well.

2 Line base and sides of a 23cm (9¼-inch) square cake pan with baking paper, extending the paper 5cm (2 inches) over the sides.

3 Place coconut on its side on a chopping board; carefully cut off the dome-shaped top with a cleaver or large knife – you will need to use a bit of force. Drain coconut water into a large jug (reserve coconut water for another use). Spoon out the soft coconut flesh; you should have about ½ cup (90g).

4 Process drained cashews and almonds until finely chopped. Add dates, shredded coconut, ¼ cup of the crystallised ginger, ¼ cup of the oil and 1 tablespoon of the syrup; pulse until combined. Press mixture over base of pan. Refrigerate until required.

5 Blend or process fresh coconut, fresh ginger, coconut milk, vanilla, remaining oil, remaining syrup and ¼ cup of the crystallised ginger until smooth. Pour mixture over biscuit base. Refrigerate slice overnight.

6 Cut slice into pieces; serve topped with flaked almonds and remaining crystallised ginger.

Banoffee pie

IF YOU HAVE ONE, USE A HIGH-POWERED BLENDER IN STEP 5; THIS TYPE OF BLENDER WILL PRODUCE A VERY SMOOTH CONSISTENCY FOR THE PIE FILLING.

You will need to start this recipe the day before.

- ¾ cup (90g) pecans
- 250g (8 ounces) vegan biscuits
- ½ cup (115g) coconut oil, at room temperature
- 1 tablespoon cacao powder
- 12 fresh dates (230g), pitted
- ⅓ cup (50g) coconut sugar
- 1 tablespoon water
- 1 tablespoon cornflour (cornstarch)
- 270ml canned coconut cream
- 1 teaspoon vanilla extract
- 3 medium bananas (600g)
- 300g (9½ ounces) silken tofu
- 2 tablespoons pure maple syrup
- ½ teaspoon ground cinnamon

1 Place pecans in a small bowl; cover with cold water. Stand for 1 hour; drain.

2 Meanwhile, process biscuits, coconut oil, cacao and half the dates until fine crumbs form and mixture starts to clump. Press biscuit mixture over base and side of a 24cm (9½-inch) fluted tart tin. Refrigerate until required.

3 Stir coconut sugar and the water in a small saucepan over low heat until sugar dissolves. Bring to the boil; boil for 3 minutes or until sugar mixture reduces slightly.

4 Meanwhile, whisk cornflour and coconut cream in a small bowl. Gradually stir coconut cream mixture into sugar syrup until smooth; cook, stirring, for 10 minutes or until mixture boils and thickens.

5 Blend drained pecans and warm coconut mixture with remaining dates, vanilla and 1 banana until as smooth as possible (see tips). Spoon mixture into biscuit case; smooth surface. Refrigerate overnight.

6 Blend or process tofu, syrup and cinnamon until smooth.

7 Thinly slice remaining bananas; arrange slices on pie. Serve pie drizzled with tofu mixture.

TIP If you aren't using a high-powdered blender, continually scrape down the sides of the blender jug to get as smooth a consistency as is possible.

SERVING IDEAS Serve with coarsely chopped pecans and dulce de leche (see page 272) drizzled over just before serving.

Tahini caramel choco cups

UNHULLED TAHINI WILL PROVIDE YOU WITH MORE MINERALS AND VITAMINS THAN THE HULLED VERSION AND ALSO A STRONGER SESAME TASTE.

- 1 cup (150g) raw cashews
- 3 cups (750ml) water
- 220g (7 ounces) dried dates, chopped coarsely
- ⅓ cup (45g) coconut butter
- ¼ cup (65g) unhulled tahini
- ⅓ cup (80ml) pure maple syrup
- 1 teaspoon salt flakes
- ¼ cup (60ml) water, extra

BASE

- 220g (7 ounces) dried dates, chopped coarsely
- 1 cup (140g) macadamias, chopped coarsely
- 2 tablespoons cacao nibs

CHOC LAYER

- ½ cup (80g) coconut butter
- ½ cup (125ml) pure maple syrup
- ½ cup (50g) cacao powder
- 1 vanilla bean, split lengthways, seeds scraped
- 2 tablespoons hot water

1 Place cashews and the water in a medium bowl, stand, covered, for 2 hours. Drain cashews, rinse under cold water; drain well.
2 Grease a 12-hole (⅓-cup/80ml) muffin pan; line each hole with two strips of baking paper crossed over one another.
3 Make base.
4 Press rounded tablespoons of base mixture firmly into each pan hole. Refrigerate until required.
5 To make caramel, process drained cashews, dates, coconut butter, tahini, syrup, salt and the extra water until smooth. Spoon rounded tablespoons of the caramel mixture equally among the bases; using wet fingers, level surface.
6 Make choc layer.
7 Spoon rounded teaspoons of choc layer over caramel; using a hot wet spoon, spread chocolate evenly. Freeze for 40 minutes or until firm.
8 Gently loosen cups from side of the pan holes with a hot palette knife; remove cups by lifting the baking paper strips.

base Process dates until a coarse paste forms. Add macadamias and cacao nibs; pulse until chopped coarsely.

choc layer Stir coconut butter and syrup in a small saucepan over medium heat until melted. Remove from heat. Add cacao powder, vanilla bean seeds and the hot water; whisk to combine.

TIP Coconut butter is the processed flesh of coconut. It is available from health food stores.
SERVING IDEAS Serve with rosemary flowers or other edible flowers scattered over the top, if available.

Chia pastry

OPT FOR A PLAIN VEGAN PASTRY
OR CHOOSE A SPICED OR
CHOCOLATE VARIATION.

- 1 tablespoon white chia seeds
- ¼ cup (60ml) water
- 1⅔ cups (250g) plain (all-purpose) flour
- 3 teaspoons caster (superfine) sugar
- 1 teaspoon sea salt flakes
- ½ cup (125ml) olive oil
- 2 tablespoons soda water, approximately

1 Pound chia seeds with a mortar and pestle or grind in a spice grinder until finely ground. Combine ground chia and the water in a small jug; stand for 30 minutes.
2 Process flour, sugar, salt, chia mixture, oil and enough of the soda water to make ingredients just come together to form a moist crumble. Turn dough onto a bench; knead lightly until smooth. Form into a disc; enclose in plastic wrap. Refrigerate for 30 minutes.
3 Roll pastry between sheets of baking paper until large enough to line a greased 24cm (9½-inch) loose-based flan tin. Lift pastry into tin; ease into side, trim edge. Refrigerate for 30 minutes.
4 Preheat oven to 180°C/350°F. Place tin on an oven tray; line pastry with baking paper; fill pastry with dried beans or uncooked rice. Bake for 15 minutes. Remove paper and weights carefully from tin; bake a further 10 minutes or until pastry is browned lightly. Cool.

TIPS Pastry is best made on day of serving. Recipe makes enough pastry to line a 24cm (9½-inch) tart tin.

vanilla & spice chia pastry Add 2 tablespoons ground mixed spice and seeds from 1 vanilla bean to flour mixture.

chocolate chia pastry Add 2 tablespoons cocoa powder to flour mixture.

Choc–cherry coconut bars

GOOD-QUALITY BRANDS OF DARK CHOCOLATE WITH
70% COCOA SOLIDS ARE OFTEN VEGAN; CHECK THE LABEL
TO ENSURE THEY DON'T CONTAIN WHEY OR CASEIN.

- **200g (6½ ounces) vegan dark chocolate (70% cocoa) (see tip), chopped coarsely**
- **1 cup (150g) dried cherries, chopped finely**
- **3 cups (240g) desiccated coconut**
- **½ cup (125ml) rice malt syrup**
- **1 teaspoon vanilla extract**
- **⅓ cup (80ml) melted coconut oil**

1 Line base and sides of an 18cm x 28cm (7¼-inch x 11¼-inch) slice pan with baking paper.

2 Place half the chocolate in a small heatproof bowl over a saucepan of gently simmering water (don't allow bowl to touch water); stir until just melted. Pour chocolate into pan; spread to cover base. Refrigerate for 15 minutes or until set. Keep water at a gentle simmer; reserve bowl off the heat.

3 Combine cherries and coconut in a large bowl; stir in syrup, vanilla and oil until combined. Press mixture very firmly in an even layer over chocolate.

4 Return pan of water to a gentle simmer over medium heat. Place remaining chocolate in reserved bowl over water; stir until melted. Pour chocolate over cherry-coconut layer; spread evenly with a spatula. Freeze for 1 hour or until set (alternatively, refrigerate for 3 hours or until set). Cut into squares before serving.

TIP Lindt and Green & Black brand dark chocolate, available from supermarkets, are vegan, plus you will also find a wide array of vegan chocolate at health food stores.

Sri Lankan Christmas cakes

TO FINELY GRIND THE CASHEWS, PULSE IN A FOOD PROCESSOR. FINISHED CAKES WILL KEEP IN AN AIRTIGHT CONTAINER FOR UP TO 2 WEEKS.

- ¼ cup (60ml) brandy
- ¼ cup (60ml) rosewater
- 2 teaspoons vanilla extract
- ½ cup (90g) white chia seeds
- 1½ cups (375ml) boiling water
- ½ cup (125ml) extra virgin olive oil
- ½ cup (110g) coconut oil, melted
- 400g (12½ ounces) canned chickpeas (garbanzo beans)
- 300g (9½ ounces) raw cashews, roasted, ground finely (see note above)
- 250g (8 ounces) medjool dates, pitted, chopped finely
- 100g (3 ounces) dried moist figs, stems removed, chopped finely
- 100g (3 ounces) dried cranberries
- 100g (3 ounces) sultanas
- 100g (3 ounces) crystallised ginger, chopped finely
- 1 teaspoon grated orange rind
- 250g (8 ounces) fine semolina
- 2 teaspoons ground cinnamon
- 1 teaspoon ground cardamom
- ¼ teaspoon ground nutmeg
- ¼ teaspoon ground cloves
- 1 teaspoon baking powder
- 1 cup (220g) firmly packed brown sugar
- freeze-dried raspberry powder, optional

CASHEW MARZIPAN

- 250g (8 ounces) cashews, roasted lightly
- 250g (8 ounces) icing (confectioners') sugar
- 1 teaspoon finely grated lemon rind
- ¼ cup (60ml) lemon juice, approximately

1 Stir brandy, rosewater, vanilla, chia and the boiling water with a small whisk in a small bowl; stand 30 minutes for liquid to thicken. Stir in oils.

2 Drain liquid (aquafaba) from chickpeas into a measuring jug; you will need approximately ¾ cup (180ml). Transfer measured liquid to large bowl of an electric mixer. Coarsely chop ½ cup of the chickpeas; reserve remainder for another use. Combine chopped chickpeas with cashews, dried fruits, ginger and rind in a large bowl.

3 Place semolina in a heavy-based frying pan; stir constantly over medium heat, for 10 minutes or until pale golden; cool. Stir in spices and baking powder. Add semolina mixture to fruit mixture. Using your hands, combine well, separating clumped pieces of fruit.

4 Preheat oven to 150°C/300°F. Grease two 6-hole (¾-cup/180ml) texas muffin pans; line base of holes with rounds of baking paper.

5 Beat measured aquafaba for 4 minutes or until soft peaks form. Gradually add sugar, beating until dissolved between additions. Add chia seed mixture and one third of the 'meringue' to fruit mixture; stir well to combine. Gently fold in remaining 'meringue'. Divide batter among pan holes.; mixture will fill holes.

6 Bake for 1 hour, swapping trays on shelves halfway through cooking time, or until a skewer inserted into the centre comes out clean. Cool cakes in pans. Gently lift cakes from pan.

7 Meanwhile, make cashew marzipan.

8 Cut marzipan into 12 portions; roll out one portion between sheets of baking paper. Cut out an 8.5cm (3½-inch) round; place on a cake. Repeat with remaining marzipan. Scraps can be used to cut decorative shapes, if desired. Mix with raspberry powder, if you like, to achieve desired pink colour. Roll out, then cut out 12 stars. Place one on each cake and sprinkle with extra raspberry powder.

cashew marzipan Process nuts, sugar and rind until finely ground. Add juice; process, scraping down the side of the bowl occasionally, until mixture forms a ball. Shape into a disc.

Berry basket cream tarts

THESE LUSCIOUS NUT-CREAM FILLED TARTS ARE THE ANSWER TO ALL VEGAN DREAMS OF BEING ABLE TO EAT A BEAUTIFUL CREAMY FRENCH FRUIT TART.

You will need to start this recipe at least 4 hours ahead.

- **2 cups (320g) natural almonds**
- **¾ cup (100g) pitted medjool dates**
- **20g (¾ ounce) coconut oil, melted**
- **1 tablespoon psyllium husks**
- **1-2 tablespoons coconut water, approximately**
- **125g (4 ounces) raspberries**
- **½ cup (65g) small strawberries, halved**
- **½ cup (75g) blueberries**
- **½ cup (100g) cherries, halved**
- **¼ cup edible flowers, optional**

PASTRY CREAM

- **2½ cups (350g) raw macadamias**
- **⅔ cup (160ml) agave syrup**
- **¾ cup (180ml) coconut water**
- **2 teaspoons finely grated orange rind**
- **2 teaspoons vanilla paste**
- **¾ cup (150g) coconut oil, melted**

1 Preheat oven to 160°C/325°F. Grease six 12cm (4¾-inch) pie dishes; line bases and sides with two strips of baking paper to form a cross, extending strips over sides.

2 Make pastry cream.

3 Process almonds, dates, oil, psyllium husks and enough coconut water until mixture forms a coarse paste and clumps together.

4 Press ⅓ cup of nut mixture firmly over base and side of each dish. Place dishes on a large oven tray. Bake for 15 minutes or until browned lightly; cool.

5 Carefully remove tart cases from dishes; place on a large tray. Divide pastry cream between cases. Cover, refrigerate for 4 hours or overnight until set.

6 Serve tarts topped with fruit and sprinkled with flowers, if you like.

pastry cream Place macadamias in a medium bowl; cover with cold water. Stand for for 4 hours or overnight; drain. Rinse macadamias; drain well. Place macadamias into the jug of a high-powered blender with remaining ingredients; blend until smooth.

DO-AHEAD Tarts can be made a day ahead; keep covered in the fridge and decorate with berries and flowers, if you like, just before serving.

Beetroot monster munch balls

LUCUMA POWDER, FROM A PERUVIAN FRUIT, HAS A CREAMY, CITRUS FLAVOUR. IT'S AVAILABLE FROM SOME HEALTH FOOD STORES OR CAN BE ORDERED ONLINE.

- 1 cup (160g) natural almonds
- 1 cup (140g) dried dates, pitted
- 2 large beetroot (beets) (400g), peeled, grated finely
- ½ cup (60g) goji berries
- ¼ cup (40g) chia seeds
- ¼ cup (25g) cacao powder
- ¼ cup (35g) lucuma powder (see note above)
- 1 tablespoon psyllium husks
- ½ cup (80g) activated buckinis
- ¼ cup (90g) rice malt syrup
- freeze-dried raspberries, optional

1 Process almonds and dates until a slightly coarse crumb forms; transfer to a large bowl. Add remaining ingredients, except raspberries; mix well with your hands until combined. You may like to use disposable gloves to protect your hands from staining.

2 Roll 1 tablespoon of mixture into a ball; roll in crushed freeze-dried raspberries, if you like. You will need to press the rapberry into the side of the ball slightly to help it stick. Place onto a tray; repeat with remaining mixture.

3 Cover; refrigerate for 4 hours or until firm. Transfer to an airtight container.

TIPS The protein balls are a perfect snack on the go, or can be served for morning or afternoon tea with herbal tea or freshly squeezed juice. They also make a great pre- or post-workout snack.

MIX IT UP The balls can be rolled in crushed freeze-dried raspberries, chopped nuts such as pistachios, sifted cacao powder, goji berries or toasted shredded coconut.

DO-AHEAD Balls will keep in the fridge for up to 1 week in an airtight container or can be frozen for up to 2 months; they can be eaten straight from the freezer.

Cashew cinnamon iced coffee

USE A GOOD DECAF COFFEE OR DANDELION COFFEE FOR A CAFFEINE-FREE OPTION, IF PREFERRED.

*You will need to begin this recipe
4 hours or a day ahead.*

- **3 cups (750ml) coconut water**
- **1 cup (150g) raw cashews**
- **⅓ cup (80ml) espresso (see tips)**
- **1 teaspoon vanilla bean paste**
- **10 fresh dates (230g), pitted**
- **½ teaspoon ground cinnamon**
- **1 tablespoon raw cashews, extra**
- **ice-cubes, to serve**

1 Pour coconut water into ice cube trays; freeze 4 hours or until firm (see tips).
2 Place cashews in a small bowl; cover with filtered water. Stand, covered, for 4 hours or overnight. Drain cashews; rinse under cold water; drain well.
3 Blend cashews in a high-powered blender with espresso, vanilla, 6 of the dates, cinnamon and a pinch of sea salt until smooth. Add coconut water ice cubes; blend until smooth.
4 Serve in glasses, topped with extra cashews and halved remaining dates.

TIPS If you don't have a coffee machine, you can purchase two espressos from a café, or make strong coffee with a plunger. If you don't have enough ice-cube trays to freeze the coconut water, pour it into a shallow tray and freeze until firm. Break into pieces before blending.

Rice pudding with poached rhubarb & plums

USE ANY DAIRY-FREE MILK, EXCEPT ALMOND MILK OAT MILK IS A GOOD CHOICE, AS IS COCONUT MILK; THOUGH YOU MAY NEED A LITTLE MORE, AS IT IS THICKER.

- 2 tablespoons pistachios
- 3 medium oranges (720g)
- 2 tablespoons vegan margarine spread
- ¾ cup (160g) sushi rice
- 1 litre (4 cups) oat milk or other dairy-free milk (see note above)
- ⅓ cup (80ml) coconut syrup
- 2 teaspoons vanilla bean paste

POACHED RHUBARB & PLUMS
- 1 litre (4 cups) apple juice
- 2 tablespoons coconut syrup
- 1 cinnamon stick
- 4 star anise
- 3 large stems rhubarb (300g), trimmed, cut into 7cm (2¾-inch) lengths
- 4 small blood plums (300g), quartered, seeded

1 Make poached rhubarb and plums.

2 Meanwhile, preheat oven to 180°C/350°F. Spread pistachios on an oven tray; roast for 5 minutes or until browned lightly. (Or, place nuts in a frying pan, toast nuts over low-medium heat, stirring, until browned lightly.)

3 Remove rind from one of the oranges using a zester. (Or, peel rind thinly from orange, avoiding white pith. Cut rind into long thin strips.) Squeeze juice from oranges; you will need 1 cup.

4 Melt spread in a large deep frying pan over a medium heat. Add rice; cook, stirring, for 2 minutes. Add juice, oat milk, coconut syrup and vanilla; bring to the boil. Reduce heat; simmer. Cook, uncovered, stirring occasionally, for 20 minutes or until the rice is tender and the mixture is thick.

5 Spoon rice mixture into six 1½ cup (375 ml) bowls. Serve topped with poached fruit and fruit syrup; sprinkled with roasted pistachios and rind.

poached rhubarb & plums Bring juice, coconut syrup and spices to a simmer in a medium saucepan over medium heat. Add rhubarb and plums; simmer, uncovered, for 2 minutes. Be careful not to boil the fruit or it will be mushy. Remove fruit from pan with a slotted spoon; transfer to a heatproof bowl. Peel plums and discard skin. Bring syrup to the boil, then reduce heat and simmer, uncovered, for 30 minutes or until reduced to 1 cup. Cool slightly. Serve warm.

TIPS If the stems of the rhubarb are thin reduce the cooking time. Serve for dessert or brunch.

DO-AHEAD Rice pudding and poached fruit can be made a day ahead; keep refrigerated, separately. Reheat the rice pudding with a little more oat milk to give a creamy mixture.

Strawberry meringues with coconut cream

BUY A QUALITY UNHOMOGENISED COCONUT CREAM, WITHOUT STABILISERS; IT WILL HAVE A THICK LAYER OF COCONUT CREAM ON TOP OF THINNER COCONUT MILK.

You will need to start this recipe a day ahead.

- **2 x 270ml cans coconut cream (see note above)**
- **½ cup (125ml) aquafaba (liquid from canned chickpeas, see tips)**
- **¾ cup (165g) caster (superfine) sugar**
- **1 teaspoon vanilla bean paste**
- **¼ teaspoon cream of tartar**
- **¼ cup (40g) icing (confectioners') sugar, sifted**
- **2 teaspoons freeze-dried strawberry or raspberry powder**
- **250g (8 ounces) strawberries, sliced**
- **15g (½ ounce) freeze-dried strawberries, crushed**
- **½ cup (65g) raspberries**
- **½ cup unsprayed edible flowers, optional**

1 Place coconut cream cans in the refrigerator overnight; don't shake or turn cans.

2 Preheat oven to 100°C/212°F. Line two large oven trays with baking paper.

3 Whisk or beat aquafaba in a small bowl with an electric stand mixer on high speed until firm peaks form, about 8 minutes (a hand beater will take longer). Gradually add sugar, whisking until dissolved between additions; whisk until thick and glossy, about 10 minutes. Quickly beat in vanilla and cream of tartar on low speed until just combined.

4 Spoon meringue mixture into a piping bag with a 1cm (½-inch) plain tube. Pipe eight 10cm (4-inch) wide, 2.5cm (1-inch) high heart-shaped meringues onto trays, 5cm (2 inches) apart. (Alternatively, using a large metal spoon, drop eight meringues into trays.) Bake for 2 hours 40 minutes or until crisp. Turn oven off; leave meringues to cool in oven overnight with door closed.

5 Without shaking, turn cans of coconut cream upside down; open cans. Drain off the thin coconut milk into a jug without disturbing the top layer. Spoon off the thick top layer of coconut cream; you will need about 1 cup. Gently whisk cream in a small bowl with sifted icing sugar and berry powder with a balloon whisk until soft peaks form. Don't over-beat or mixture will be grainy.

6 Just before serving, spoon cream mixture onto meringues. Served topped with both strawberries, raspberries and edible flowers, if you like.

TIPS You can use leftover coconut milk in smoothies, curries, baking or on cereal. Aquafaba is the drained liquid from canned legumes. A 420g (13½-ounce) can generally provide ½ cup aquafaba. We recommend using chickpea liquid for this recipe, so that it doesn't colour the meringues. You can keep aquafaba in the fridge for 2 days or freeze for up to 3 months.

DO-AHEAD Meringues will keep in an airtight container for a week.

Rich chocolate & ginger mousse with semi-dried figs

WE HAVE USED AQUAFABA, THE DRAINED LIQUID FROM CANNED LEGUMES IN PLACE OF EGG WHITES. A 420G (13½-OUNCE) CAN GENERALLY PROVIDES ½ CUP AQUAFABA.

- 200g (6½ ounces) vegan dark chocolate (70% cocoa), chopped
- ⅓ cup (80ml) water
- 2 teaspoons vanilla bean paste
- ½ teaspoon ground ginger
- ½ cup (125ml) aquafaba (liquid from canned legumes, see note above)
- ¾ cup (165g) caster (superfine) sugar
- 1 teaspoon cacao powder
- 2 tablespoons slivered pistachios

SEMI-DRIED FIGS
- 6 small fresh figs (300g)
- 2 tablespoons caster (superfine) sugar
- ¼ teaspoon ground ginger

1 Make semi-dried figs.

2 Meanwhile, place chocolate, the water, vanilla and ginger in a heatproof bowl over a saucepan of simmering water. Stir until melted and smooth.

3 Whisk or beat aquafaba in a small bowl with an electric mixer on high speed for 8 minutes or until firm peaks form. Gradually add sugar, whisking until dissolved between additions; whisk until thick and glossy. Working quickly, fold one-third of the aquafaba mixture into chocolate mixture, then fold in remaining mixture. Spoon into six ¾-cup (180ml) glasses. Cover, refrigerate for 30 minutes or until set.

4 Serve mousse dusted with sifted cacao powder and topped with semi-dried figs and pistachios.

semi-dried figs Preheat oven to 120°C/250°F. Line an oven tray with baking paper. Halve figs lengthways; place on tray cut-side up. Sprinkle with sugar and ginger. Bake for 4 hours or until semi-dried; cool.

SWAP Use cocoa powder if you don't have cacao.

DO-AHEAD You can make semi-dried figs a day ahead; store in an airtight container at room temperature. You can make the mousse a day ahead, cover with plastic wrap and refrigerate until required.

Fudgy sweet potato brownies with espresso sauce

GRIND THE LINSEED (FLAXSEED) YOURSELF, OR BUY IT FROM STORES WITH A GOOD TURNOVER, AS GROUND LINSEED TURNS RANCID QUITE QUICKLY.

- **1 medium orange sweet potato (400g), peeled, chopped**
- **2 tablespoons ground linseed (flax meal)**
- **½ cup (125ml) hot water**
- **180g (5½ ounces) vegan dark chocolate (70% cocoa), chopped**
- **1¼ cups (200g) coconut sugar**
- **2 teaspoons vanilla extract**
- **¼ cup (60ml) water, extra**
- **2 tablespoons cacao powder**
- **1 cup (120g) almond meal**
- **¼ teaspoon bicarbonate of soda (baking soda)**

ESPRESSO SAUCE
- **2 teaspoons instant coffee granules**
- **1 tablespoon boiling water**
- **⅓ cup (80ml) pure maple syrup**
- **⅓ cup (55g) coconut sugar**
- **20g (¾ ounce) vegan dark chocolate (70% cocoa), chopped**
- **¼ cup (50g) coconut oil**
- **2 teaspoons vanilla extract**
- **¼ cup (25g) cacao powder**

1 Place sweet potato in a medium saucepan with enough cold water to cover; bring to the boil. Cook, covered, for 15 minutes or until soft. Drain; return to saucepan. Mash until smooth.

2 Meanwhile, preheat oven to 180°C/350°F. Lightly grease a deep 20cm (8-inch) square cake pan; line base with baking paper.

3 Combine ground linseed and the hot water in a small heatproof bowl. Stand for 10 minutes.

4 Place chocolate, sugar, vanilla, the extra water and sifted cacao in a large heatproof bowl over a saucepan of simmering water. Stir until melted and smooth. Remove from heat; stir in mashed sweet potato. Add linseed mixture, almond meal and soda; mix well. Pour mixture into pan. Bake for 1 hour or until firm to touch. Cool slightly in pan.

5 Make espresso sauce.

6 Cut warm brownie into squares. Serve brownie with espresso sauce, topped with sweet potato peace signs, if you like (see serving idea).

espresso sauce Dissolve coffee in the boiling water. Combine syrup, sugar, chocolate, oil, vanilla and coffee in a small saucepan over low heat; stir until melted and smooth. Remove from heat; stir in sifted cacao.

TIP The sauce thickens quickly on standing. Reheat gently to return to a thin consistancy.
DO-AHEAD This brownie is also delicious at room temperature and will last for up to 3 days in an airtight container in the fridge. Bring to room temperature before serving. Brownie can also be frozen in a container for up to 2 months.
SERVING IDEA Decorate brownie squares with individual sweet potato peace signs: Peel and slice 1 small orange sweet potato (300g) into 3mm thick slices. Using a 3cm pastry cutter, cut into rounds. Heat 2 teaspoons coconut oil in a large frying pan over high heat, then cook for 2 minutes each side, until just tender. Pour in 1 tablespoon coconut syrup and cook another minute, until slightly caramelised. Cut each round into peace symbols, as pictured opposite.

Caramel coconut bread puddings

TO TOAST THE COCONUT, STIR CONTINOUSLY IN A HEAVY-BASED FRYING PAN OVER MEDIUM HEAT FOR 3 MINUTES OR UNTIL LIGHTLY BROWNED AND TOASTED.

- ½ cup (80g) coconut sugar
- 1 cup (250ml) coconut cream
- 2 tablespoons pure maple syrup
- 3 teaspoons cornflour (cornstarch)
- 2 teaspoons vanilla extract
- 2 cups (500ml) almond milk
- ½ cup (125g) apple sauce
- ½ teaspoon mixed spice
- 620g (1¼-pound) loaf wholemeal sourdough bread, crusts removed, chopped coarsely
- ⅓ cup (55g) sultanas
- ½ cup (60g) pecans
- ½ cup (25g) coconut flakes, toasted

1 Combine ⅓ cup of the sugar, ⅔ cup of the coconut cream, syrup, cornflour and half the vanilla in a small saucepan; stir until smooth. Cook, stirring, over medium heat, until mixture boils and thickens. Remove from heat.

2 Transfer half the coconut mixture to a large heatproof jug. Gradually stir in milk, sauce, spice and remaining vanilla.

3 Preheat oven to 180°C/350°F. Grease an 8-cup, 22cm (8½-inch) x 30cm (12-inch) baking dish. Layer bread, sultanas and pecans in dish. Pour milk mixture over bread, making sure all the bread is soaked. Stand for 15 minutes.

4 Sprinkle bread with remaining sugar. Bake pudding for 40 minutes or until set.

5 Serve pudding warm or cooled, with reserved caramel sauce, remaining coconut cream and coconut flakes.

TIP If reserved caramel sauce becomes a little thick on standing, stir in some extra coconut cream or almond milk and reheat gently over low heat to return to a sauce consistency.

PREP TIME 20 MINUTES (+ COOLING & FREEZING)
MAKES 1.5 LITRES (6 CUPS)

Ice-cream sandwiches

chunky monkey coco-cream Place 1 cup (150g) raw cashews in a medium heatproof bowl, pour over 1 cup boiling water; stand until cooled. Drain. Blend cashews, 2 chopped ripe bananas (340g) and 2 tablespoons lemon juice until smooth. Add 270ml canned coconut milk, ⅔ cup (160ml) pure maple syrup, 1 teaspoon sea salt and all but 2 tablespoons of a 375g (12 ounces) jar natural peanut butter; blend until smooth. Pour into a 20cm (8-inch) square cake tin. Cover; freeze overnight until firm. Turn ice-cream out onto a chopping board; chop into pieces. Blend until smooth. Wash and dry cake tin; line base and sides with baking paper, extending paper slightly beyond tin rim. Return ice-cream to tin, dot over remaining peanut butter, add 50g (1½oz) chopped dark chocolate and ¼ cup (35g) chopped roasted peanuts; stir to swirl through. Freeze for a further hour or until firm again. Lift ice-cream from tin. Cut into 4 rounds. Sandwich ice-cream between vegan biscuits, top with extra chopped chocolate and peanuts, or serve in scoops.

raspberry almond coco-cream Make chunky monkey coco-cream above with the following substitutions: Substitute 200g (6½oz) jar almond butter for peanut butter. (There's no need to reserve any almond butter.) Omit the chocolate and peanuts; instead stir in 1½ cups (225g) fresh or thawed frozen raspberries. Cut into 4 rounds. Sandwich ice-cream between vegan biscuits, top with extra raspberries, if you like, or serve in scoops.

key lime pie coco-cream Make chunky monkey coco-cream above with the following substitutions: Replace lemon juice with ¼ cup (60ml) lime juice, maple syrup with ⅔ cup (180ml) rice malt syrup and peanut butter with 375g (12oz) dairy-free coconut yoghurt; add 3 teaspoons finely grated lime rind. Omit the chocolate and peanuts. Cut into 4 rounds. Sandwich ice-cream between vegan biscuits or serve in scoops.

Summer fruit parcels

THIS IS A SIMPLE WAY OF COOKING THAT EXTRACTS AND MELDS ALL THE SUNNY FLAVOURS OF PRIME STONE FRUIT IN WHAT IS ESSENTIALLY A STEAMING COOKING METHOD.

- **2 medium peaches (300g), quartered, stones removed**
- **2 medium nectarines (340g), quartered, stones removed**
- **4 medium plums (450g), halved, stones removed**
- **1 teaspoon vanilla bean paste**
- **¼ teaspoon mixed spice**
- **¼ cup (60ml) vegan marsala or other fortified wine**
- **2 tablespoons coconut sugar**
- **2 tablespoons coconut flakes, toasted**
- **2 tablespoons slivered almonds, toasted**

1 Preheat oven to 200°C/400°F. Cut four 30cm (12-inch) squares of baking paper.
2 Combine fruit, vanilla, spice, wine and sugar in a large bowl; toss to combine. Stand for 15 minutes; toss gently.
3 Divide fruit evenly among squares. Pour syrup over fruit. Bring in edges of paper to the centre to form a parcel, using kitchen string to secure. Place parcels on an oven tray; bake for 30 minutes or until fruit is just tender.
4 Serve fruit sprinkled with coconut flakes and almonds.

TIP To toast coconut and almonds, stir continuously in a heavy-based frying pan over medium heat until lightly browned.
SERVING IDEAS Serve with vegan yoghurt or soy ice-cream, such as a coconut flavoured one.

Raspberry & mango paletas

INTENSELY FRUITY AND REFRESHING, PALETAS ARE MEXICO'S ANSWER TO ICY POLES. TO CAPTURE THE FRUIT'S BEST FLAVOUR, CHOOSE A RIPE MANGO.

- 250g (8 ounces) raspberries
- ½ cup (125ml) coconut milk
- ⅓ cup (80ml) pure maple syrup
- 2 tablespoons lemon juice
- 1 large mango (600g), chopped coarsely
- 1 teaspoon vanilla extract
- 1 cup (80g) desiccated coconut, toasted, optional

1 Blend or process raspberries and coconut milk until smooth. Transfer to a small bowl; stir in ¼ cup of the maple syrup and half the juice.

2 Pour mixture into ten ⅓-cup (80ml) ice block moulds, then insert stick. Freeze for about 4 hours or until firm.

3 Blend or process mango until smooth. Transfer to a small bowl; stir in vanilla, remaining syrup and juice.

4 Pour mixture over raspberry layer in ice block moulds. Freeze for 4 hours or until set.

5 Remove paletas from freezer. Stand for 5 minutes before removing from moulds. Serve with bowls of desiccated coconut for dipping, if you like.

DO-AHEAD The paletas will keep in the freezer for 1 month.

Apples & pears with walnut miso caramel

THE NEW FLAVOUR MAKER TO HIT THE KITCHEN IN CARAMEL SAUCES IS UMAMI-RICH MISO, AND OUR VERSION DOES THE TRICK, MINUS CREAM AND BUTTER.

- 3 small red apples (400g), halved lengthways, skin on, stems on (see tips)
- 3 small pears (540g), halved crossways, skin on, stems on (see tips)
- 2 tablespoons orange juice
- 2 tablespoons dark brown sugar
- 150g (4½ ounces) blackberries
- 125g (4 ounces) raspberries

WALNUT MISO CARAMEL
- ½ cup (110g) firmly packed dark brown sugar
- 2 tablespoons white (shiro) miso
- 1 teaspoon ground cinnamon
- 1 cup (100g) walnuts, roasted
- ½ cup (125ml) fresh orange juice

1 Preheat oven to 200°C/400°F. Line two shallow-sided oven trays with baking paper.

2 Toss fruit with juice and sugar in a medium bowl; divide between trays. Roast fruit for 25 minutes, turning occasionally, or until just tender (see tips).

3 Meanwhile, make walnut miso caramel.

4 Serve roasted fruit drizzled with caramel, topped with berries and remaining walnuts.

walnut miso caramel Combine sugar, miso, cinnamon, half of the walnuts and juice in a medium saucepan over high heat; bring to the boil. Reduce heat; simmer, stirring occasionally, for 5 minutes or until thickened slightly.

TIPS Keep an eye on the cooking time of the apples and pears, as it will differ depending on the size and ripeness of the fruit. The fruit is done when you can insert a knife easily without resistance. Larger fruit needs to be quartered rather than halved and very small apples (70g each) (2½ ounces) can be pierced through the base and sides with a fork before baking whole.
Caramel will thicken on standing; reheat gently if needed and serve warm.

Cacao hazelnut cookies with 'cookie dough' topping

YOU GET A DOUBLE DOSE OF 'COOKIE' WITH THESE TREATS; FIRST THE COOKED CHOCOLATEY BASE, THEN A NAUGHTY RAW COOKIE DOUGH-TASTING TOPPING.

- 1⅓ cups (400g) mashed banana (see tip)
- ⅔ cup (180g) cashew spread
- 1 cup (100g) hazelnut meal
- ⅓ cup (35g) cacao powder
- 2 tablespoons pure maple syrup
- 2 cups (180g) rolled oats
- 1 teaspoon finely grated orange rind
- ⅓ cup (70g) coarsely chopped roasted hazelnuts

'COOKIE DOUGH' TOPPING

- ⅓ cup (80ml) coconut oil, melted
- ⅓ cup (80ml) pure maple syrup
- 1 teaspoon vanilla bean paste
- ⅔ cup (90g) white spelt flour
- ⅓ cup (35g) hazelnut meal

1 Preheat oven to 180°C/350°F. Line two large baking trays with baking paper.

2 Combine ingredients, except chopped hazelnuts, in a medium bowl.

3 Roll heaped tablespoons of mixture into balls. Place on trays about 5cm (2 inches) apart. With slightly damp hands, press down on balls of mixture until 6cm (2½-inch) round.

4 Bake for 12 minutes or until when gently pushed cookie moves without breaking. Transfer cookies to a wire rack to cool.

5 Make 'cookie dough' topping.

6 Serve cookies topped with 'cookie dough' topping; sprinkle with chopped hazelnuts.

'cookie dough' topping Combine ingredients in a medium bowl.

TIP You will need about 4 medium (800g) overripe bananas for this recipe.
DO-AHEAD These cookies will last up to 3 days in an airtight container at room temperature, or freeze for up to 2 months.

Watermelon & cherries in mojito syrup

THIS REFRESHING SALAD CAN ALSO BE PULLED TOGETHER WITH OTHER FRUIT COMBINATIONS, SUCH AS PINEAPPLE AND MANGO, OR PEACHES AND STRAWBERRIES.

- **2 medium limes (180g)**
- **½ cup (125ml) light agave syrup**
- **¼ cup (60ml) white rum**
- **2 tablespoons finely chopped fresh mint leaves**
- **2 cups (300g) fresh cherries, halved**
- **400g (12½ ounces) seedless watermelon, chopped coarsely or thinly sliced and cut into 3cm (1¼-inch) stars**
- **coconut ice-cream , to serve**
- **fresh small mint leaves, extra**

CANDIED LIME PEPITA BRITTLE
- **⅓ cup (80ml) light agave syrup**
- **⅓ cup (75g) caster (superfine) sugar**
- **2 teaspoons finely grated lime rind**
- **⅓ cup (65g) pepitas (pumpkin seed kernels)**

1 Remove rind from 1 lime using a zester (or, peel rind thinly from lime, avoiding white pith; cut rind into long thin strips). Squeeze juice from zested lime; you will need 1 tablespoon. Place zest, syrup and 2 tablespoons of the rum in a small saucepan; bring to the boil. Simmer, uncovered, for 2 minutes or until thickened slightly. Stir in mint. Remove from heat; strain and stir in cherries, remaining rum and juice. Cool.

2 Combine watermelon and cherries syrup in a large bowl. Cover; refrigerate for 1 hour.

3 Meanwhile, make candied lime pepita brittle.

4 Thinly slice remaining lime. Serve fruit and syrup with ice-cream and lime slices, sprinkled with pieces of brittle and extra mint leaves.

candied lime pepita brittle Line an oven tray with baking paper. Place syrup and sugar in a large frying pan over low heat; stir until sugar dissolves. Bring syrup to the boil over medium heat; cook, stirring occasionally, for 5 minutes or until mixture turns a golden colour and reaches hard-crack stage. Add rind and pepitas. Pour onto tray; cool. Break into bite-sized pieces.

TIPS The brittle is best served on the day it is made as it can soften; keep it in an airtight container in a cool, dry place as soon as it has cooled.

Doughnut balls with blueberry glaze

TRY SCATTERING THE DOUGHNUT BALLS WITH A CONFETTI OF BLUEBERRY OR OTHER FRUIT POWDER AND FINELY GRATED LEMON RIND, AND EVEN CHOPPED NUTS.

- 4 teaspoons (14g) dry yeast
- ½ cup (125ml) warm water
- ¾ cup (180ml) unsweetened almond milk
- 80g (2½ ounces) vegan margarine spread, melted
- ⅓ cup (75g) caster (superfine) sugar
- 1 teaspoon sea salt
- 3 cups (450g) plain (all-purpose) flour
- vegetable oil, for deep-frying

BLUEBERRY GLAZE
- 1½ cups (240g) icing (confectioners') sugar
- ½ cup (75g) blueberries
- 2 teaspoons lemon juice
- 2 teaspoons vanilla extract

1 Combine yeast and the warm water in a small bowl. Stand for 5 minutes or until frothy.

2 Combine yeast mixture, almond milk, spread, sugar and salt in large bowl of an electric mixer fitted with a dough hook. Add flour, beat until a smooth dough forms. Place dough in a large oiled bowl; cover with plastic wrap. Stand in a warm place for 1 hour or until doubled in size.

3 Line a large oven tray with baking paper. Using a lightly floured knife, cut into 32 pieces. Roll each piece into a ball; place balls on tray, 2cm (¾-inch) apart. Cover with oiled plastic wrap. Stand in a warm place for 30 minutes or until dough has risen and is light.

4 Fill a medium saucepan one-third full with oil; heat over medium heat to 180°C/350°F (or until a cube of bread turns golden in 15 seconds). Deep-fry doughnuts, in batches, for 3 minutes or until golden and cooked through. Drain on paper towel.

5 Make blueberry glaze. Pour over doughnuts. Serve doughnuts warm or stand until cooled.

blueberry glaze Sift icing sugar into a medium bowl. Add remaining ingredients; mash blueberries with a fork. Stir until well combined. Strain glaze through a sieve.

TIP You could use soy or coconut milk instead of almond milk. These doughnuts are best served on the day they are made.

Coconut scones

IT'S HARD TO PASS UP A GOOD, SIMPLE SCONE AND THESE DON'T DISAPPOINT, JUST REMEMBER – DON'T OVERMIX THE DOUGH AND STAMP OUT, NOT TWIST, THE ROUNDS.

- **3 cups (450g) self-raising flour**
- **¼ cup (40g) icing (confectioners') sugar**
- **¾ cup (180ml) canned coconut milk**
- **1 cup (250ml) soda water**
- **1 tablespoon canned coconut milk, extra**
- **125g (4 ounces) raspberries**
- **1 teaspoon lemon juice**
- **3 teaspoons coconut sugar**
- **1 cup (280g) vegan coconut yoghurt**

1 Preheat oven to 220°C/425°F. Line an oven tray with baking paper.

2 Sift flour and icing sugar into a large bowl. Make a well in the centre; add coconut milk and soda water. Use a butter knife to "cut" the liquid through the flour mixture, mixing to a soft, sticky dough. Turn onto a lightly floured surface; knead until just smooth. Press dough out to 3cm (1¼-inch) thickness.

3 Dip a 5.5cm (2¼-inch) cutter in flour; cut 12 rounds from dough. Place scones side by side on tray, just touching. Brush tops of scones with extra coconut milk. Bake for 15 minutes or until browned and centre scones sound hollow when tapped. Leave scones on tray for 3 minutes. Transfer scones to a wire rack to cool.

4 Place berries, juice and coconut sugar in a medium bowl. Using a fork, crush raspberries. Refrigerate for 30 minutes. Drain excess liquid from raspberries over a jug or bowl.

5 Halve cooled scones; serve topped with yoghurt and berry mixture.

TIP You can use a smaller cutter and make smaller scones if you prefer; reduce the cooking time slightly.

DO-AHEAD Scones are best made on the day of serving, however, they can also be frozen for up to 2 months in a container. To thaw scones, wrap in foil and heat in the oven at 180°C/350°F for 10 minutes or until heated through.

Almond milk & mango pikelets

THIS IS NOTHING FANCY – JUST AN HONEST TO GOODNESS SWEET FIX TO WHIP UP IN MINUTES, BECAUSE SOMETIMES THAT'S ALL YOU WANT.

- 1½ cups (225g) self-raising flour
- 1 teaspoon baking powder
- 1 tablespoon golden caster (superfine) sugar
- 1½ cups (375ml) almond milk
- 1 tablespoon coconut oil, melted
- ½ teaspoon vanilla extract
- ½ cup (125ml) water
- ¼ cup (55g) firmly packed brown sugar
- 2 small mangoes (600g), sliced
- ⅓ cup (25g) natural flaked almonds, roasted, optional (see tip)

1 Sift flour, baking powder and sugar into a medium bowl. Gradually whisk in milk, oil and vanilla until smooth. Stand for 15 minutes.

2 Heat a large non-stick frying pan over medium heat. Using 2 tablespoons of batter for each pikelet, cook about four pikelets at a time, uncovered, for 2 minutes or until bubbles appear on the surface. Turn; cook until golden. Remove pikelets from pan; cover to keep warm. Repeat with remaining batter to make 12 pikelets in total.

3 Heat the water and brown sugar in a medium frying pan over low heat, stirring, until dissolved. Bring to the boil. Boil, uncovered, for 3 minutes or until mixture thickens slightly.

4 Serve pikelets with mango, sauce and almonds.

TIP Roasting nuts brings out the flavour. There are two ways to roast them: Spread nuts onto an oven tray, roast in 180°C/350°F oven for 5 to 10 minutes, or until nuts are golden brown (stir nuts once during roasting for even cooking). Or, place nuts in a heavy-based frying pan, stir nuts continuously over medium heat until browned evenly.

SERVING IDEA Serve with soy vanilla ice-cream, if you like.

Matcha mint slice

PEPPERMINT EXTRACT IS AVAILABLE FROM HEALTH FOOD STORES. BUY PEPPERMINT EXTRACT, RATHER THAN OIL OR ESSENCE, OR THE FLAVOUR WILL BE DIFFERENT.

You will need to start this recipe a day ahead.

- **2⅓ cups (350g) raw cashews**
- **¾ cup (100g) raw macadamias**
- **¾ cup (60g) desiccated coconut**
- **¾ cup (150g) coconut oil, melted**
- **2 teaspoons light agave syrup**
- **½ cup (125ml) coconut cream**
- **2 teaspoons finely grated lime rind**
- **¼ cup (60ml) lime juice**
- **½ cup (125ml) pure maple syrup**
- **1½ tablespoons matcha tea powder**
- **½ teaspoon pure peppermint extract (see note above)**

1 Place 2 cups of the cashews in a large bowl; cover with cold water. Stand, covered, for 4 hours or overnight. Drain cashews, rinse under cold water; drain well.

2 Lightly grease a 20cm (8-inch) square cake pan; line base and sides with baking paper, extending paper 5cm (2 inches) over sides.

3 Process remaining cashews and macadamias until crumbly. Add desiccated coconut, ¼ cup of the coconut oil and the agave syrup; process until mixture starts to come together. Press nut mixture firmly and evenly over base of pan, using a plastic spatula to form a 6mm (¼-inch) thick layer. Refrigerate.

4 Meanwhile, blend drained cashews and coconut cream with rind, juice, maple syrup and remaining coconut oil until as smooth as possible. Add matcha and peppermint extract; blend until combined.

5 Pour matcha mixture over base; smooth top. Cover, refrigerate overnight or until firm. Or, freeze for 3 hours or until firm.

6 Just before serving, cut slice into squares.

TIPS If you have one, use a high-powered blender in step 4; this type of blender will produce a very smooth consistency.
TO DECORATE Dust the top of the slice with a little extra matcha powder or top with desiccated coconut or chopped macadamias.
DO-AHEAD Store in an airtight container in the fridge for up to 6 days. The slice can be frozen in a container for up to 2 months. Slice is best eaten within 30 minutes of removing from freezer.

Citrus poppy seed celebration cake

HOSTING A BIRTHDAY, AFTERNOON TEA, MOTHER'S DAY OR CHRISTENING? THIS CAKE TICKS ALL THE BOXES FOR WHEN YOU NEED A SPECTACULARLY DELICIOUS CAKE.

- 1 cup (250ml) orange juice
- ⅓ cup (50g) poppy seeds
- 2 cups (500ml) canned coconut milk
- 1½ tablespoons apple cider vinegar
- 2½ cups (375g) self-raising flour
- 2 teaspoons bicarbonate of soda (baking soda)
- 2 teaspoons baking powder
- 1⅓ cups (300g) golden caster (superfine) sugar
- 2 tablespoons finely grated orange rind
- 750g (1½ pounds) vegan coconut yoghurt
- 250g (8 ounces) blueberries
- 3 teaspoons finely grated lemon rind
- 1 cup (160g) pure icing (confectioners') sugar
- 1½ tablespoons lemon juice
- edible flowers, optional

1 Preheat oven to 170°C/340°F. Grease two deep 20cm (8-inch) round cake pans; line bases and sides with baking paper.

2 Combine orange juice and seeds in a small bowl; stand for 15 minutes.

3 Meanwhile, combine coconut milk and vinegar in a medium bowl; stand for 5 minutes.

4 Sift flour, soda, baking powder and caster sugar into a large bowl. Make a well in the centre, add seed mixture, coconut milk mixture and orange rind; whisk until just combined. Divide mixture evenly between pans.

5 Bake cakes for 50 minutes or until a skewer inserted into the centre comes out clean. Cool cakes in tins for 10 minutes before turning out onto wire racks to cool.

6 Split cakes in half; refrigerate cakes for 2 hours.

7 Place one base layer of cake on a plate. Top with a quarter each of the yoghurt, blueberries and lemon rind. Repeat layering with remaining cake layers, yoghurt, blueberries and rind, finishing with the final cake layer, topped with yoghurt.

8 Sift icing sugar into a medium bowl; stir in lemon juice until smooth. Drizzle over top of cake. Top with edible flowers, if you like.

DO-AHEAD Cakes can be made to the end of step 6 a day ahead; store in an airtight container at room temperature. They can also be frozen for up to 3 months. Thaw, then continue with recipe.

SERVING IDEAS Serve cake topped with seasonal fruit, thin strips of citrus rind and edible flowers or unsprayed flowers to decorate.

Chocolate ganache cupcakes

PIMP THE CUPCAKES WITH COLOURFUL EXTRAS, SUCH AS BEETROOT POWDER AND SMASHED PISTACHIO, SQUARES OF COLOURFUL VEGAN CHOCOLATE, OR PRETTY FLOWERS

- ¾ cup (180ml) soy milk
- 2 teaspoons apple cider vinegar
- ½ cup (110g) caster (superfine) sugar
- ¼ cup (60ml) vegetable oil
- 1 teaspoon vanilla extract
- ¾ cup (110g) self-raising flour
- ¼ cup (25g) cocoa powder
- ½ teaspoon bicarbonate of soda (baking soda)
- 1 teaspoon baking powder
- ½ teaspoon salt

GANACHE
- 200g (6½ ounces) vegan dark chocolate (70% cocoa), chopped
- ¾ cup (180ml) canned coconut cream
- 1 teaspoon vanilla extract
- 1 teaspoon sea salt

1 Preheat oven to 180°C/350°F. Line a 12-hole (⅓ cup/80ml) muffin pan with paper cases.

2 Whisk soy milk and vinegar in a large bowl. Stand for 5 minutes to curdle. Add sugar, oil and vanilla to soy mixture; whisk until foamy.

3 Sift dry ingredients onto a sheet of baking paper. Sift again over milk mixture, in two batches, then whisk until almost smooth. Spoon mixture into cases. Bake for 18 minutes or until a skewer inserted into the centre comes out clean. Transfer cupcakes to a wire rack to cool.

4 Meanwhile, make ganache. Serve cupcakes topped with ganache.

ganache Place chocolate in a medium heatproof bowl over a saucepan of simmering water. Stir until chocolate is smooth; remove from heat. Stir in coconut cream, vanilla and salt. Refrigerate for 30 minutes, whisking every 10 minutes or until spreadable.

DO-AHEAD Cupcakes can be baked up 2 days ahead; store in an airtight contain at room temperature. Cupcakes, withou ganache, can be frozen for up to 3 mont SERVING IDEAS Decorate with dehydra sliced pear arranged on top of the cupca sprinkled with raspberry powder. Soak pear in raspberry juice to make them ev more decadent, if you like.

Chocolate hazelnut slice

YOUR GENEROUS DREAMILY RICH SLICE WITH LITTLE
NUBBLY POCKETS OF NUTS AND BUCKWHEAT IS INSPIRED
BY BELOVED FERRERO ROCHER CHOCOLATES.

... need to start this recipe a
... ...ad.

... ...ps (300g) raw cashews
... ...ps (280g) skinless hazelnuts
... ...up (60g) almond meal
... ...up (35g) cacao powder
... ...aspoons vanilla bean powder
... ...up (150g) activated
... ...kwheat groats
... ...up (80ml) coconut nectar
... ...up (140g) coconut oil, melted
... ...up (140g) chocolate hazelnut
... ...ter
... ...up (125ml) pure maple syrup
... ...up (60ml) coconut cream
... ...drops (about ⅛ teaspoon)
... ...ural hazelnut flavour
... ...e tips)
... ...easpoon salt

... GANACHE
... ...up (75g) cacao powder
... ...up (70g) coconut oil, melted
... ...up (180ml) pure maple syrup
... ...easpoon vanilla bean powder

1 Place cashews in a large bowl; cover
with cold water. Stand, covered, for
4 hours or overnight. Drain cashews,
rinse under cold water; drain well.
2 Lightly grease an 18cm x 28cm
(7¼-inch x 11¼-inch) slice pan; line base
and sides with baking paper, extending
paper 5cm (2-inches) over sides.
3 Process 1 cup of the hazelnuts,
almond meal, cacao powder and half the
vanilla powder until mixture resembles
coarse crumbs. Add buckwheat groats,
nectar and 2 tablespoons of the oil;
process until just combined. Press nut
mixture firmly and evenly over base
of pan, using a plastic spatula. Freeze
while preparing filling.
4 Blend drained cashews with remaining
oil, chocolate hazelnut butter, syrup,
coconut cream, remaining vanilla
powder, hazelnut flavour and salt until
as smooth as possible. Pour half the
mixture over base; smooth top.
5 Finely chop ⅔ cup of the remaining
hazelnuts; sprinkle over filling. Pour over
remaining cashew mixture; smooth top.
Cover; freeze for 3 hours or until firm.

6 Make chocolate ganache.
7 Pour chocolate ganache over slice;
smooth top. Refrigerate for 20 minutes.
8 Coarsely chop remaining hazelnuts.
Sprinkle over slice.
9 Cut slice into rectangles.
chocolate ganache Blend ingredients
until as smooth as possible.

TIPS Natural hazelnut flavour is available
from selected health food stores or can
be purchased online. Hazelnut flavour
may vary depending on the brand. We
used Medicine Flower's natural hazelnut
flavour. If using hazelnut oil or hazelnut
essence, use only 1 or 2 drops; for hazelnut
extract use about ½ teaspoon.
If you have one, use a high-speed blender
in steps 4 and 6; this type of blender will
produce a very smooth consistency.
DO-AHEAD Store in an airtight container
in the fridge for up to 6 days. The slice can
be frozen in a container for up to 2 months.
Slice is best eaten within 30 minutes of
removing from freezer.

Raw blueberry lemon un-cheesecake

BLUEBERRIES CREATE THE EXQUISITE PURPLE COLOUR OF THIS 'CHEESECAKE'. CAKE IS BEST EATEN WITHIN 30 MINUTES OF REMOVING FROM FREEZER.

You will need to start this recipe a day ahead.

- **3 cups (450g) raw cashews**
- **1 cup (140g) macadamias**
- **½ cup (40g) desiccated coconut**
- **5 fresh dates (100g), pitted**
- **½ cup (60g) pecans**
- **½ teaspoon mesquite powder (see tips)**
- **¼ teaspoon salt**
- **⅓ cup (80ml) coconut cream**
- **½ cup (125ml) light agave syrup or ⅔ cup (160ml) pure maple syrup**
- **1½ tablespoons finely grated lemon rind**
- **⅓ cup (80ml) lemon juice**
- **½ teaspoon vanilla bean powder**
- **⅔ cup (140g) coconut oil, melted**
- **40g (1½ ounces) cacao butter, melted**
- **1½ cups (225g) frozen blueberries**
- **125g (4 ounces) fresh blueberries, optional**
- **1 large lemon, sliced thinly crossways, optional**

1 Place cashews in a medium bowl; cover with cold water. Stand, covered, for 4 hours or overnight. Drain cashews, rinse under cold water; drain well.

2 Grease a 20cm (8-inch) round springform cake pan. Line base and side with baking paper.

3 Process macadamias, desiccated coconut and dates until mixture resembles coarse crumbs. Add pecans, mesquite and salt; process until combined and mixture starts to stick together. Press nut mixture firmly and evenly over base of pan using a plastic spatula. Freeze until required.

4 Blend drained cashews, coconut cream, syrup, rind, juice and vanilla powder until as smooth as possible. Add oil and cacao butter; process until well combined and completely smooth.

5 Pour two-thirds of the lemon filling over base; smooth top. Scatter with ½ cup frozen blueberries; press berries lightly into filling. Freeze for 1 hour to firm up a little.

6 Meanwhile, thaw remaining frozen blueberries. Add blueberries and any juice to remaining lemon filling; blend until as smooth as possible. Spread blueberry filling over lemon filling; smooth top. Freeze cake for 4 hours or until firm.

7 Remove cake from pan; place on a plate. Decorate with fresh blueberries, and lemon slices, if you like.

TIPS Mesquite powder is a Native American food rich in minerals with a sweet caramel-like taste; it's not critical to the recipe, so omit it if you like.

If you have one, use a high-powered blender in steps 4 and 6; this type of blender will produce a very smooth consistency.

DO-AHEAD Store cake in an airtight container in the fridge for up to 5 days. The undecorated cake can be frozen in a container for up to 2 months.

Peppermint bites

ACTIVATED BUCKWHEAT GROATS ARE AVAILABLE FROM HEALTH FOOD STORES; THEY ADD A PLEASANT CRUNCH.

You will need to start this recipe a day ahead.

- ¾ cup (115g) raw cashews
- ½ cup (80g) natural almonds
- ½ cup (60g) pecans
- ⅓ cup (65g) activated buckwheat groats (see note above)
- ⅔ cup (50g) desiccated coconut
- ½ cup (50g) cacao powder
- ¼ cup (40g) coconut sugar
- 2 teaspoons mesquite powder (see tips)
- 4 fresh dates (80g), pitted
- ⅔ cup (140g) coconut oil, melted
- ¼ cup (60ml) coconut cream
- 2 tablespoons light agave syrup
- ½ teaspoon pure peppermint extract (see tips)

CHOCOLATE COATING

- ¼ cup (50g) coconut oil
- 60g (2 ounces) cacao butter, chopped
- 2 tablespoons pure maple syrup
- ½ cup (50g) cacao powder

1 Place cashews in a medium bowl; cover with cold water. Stand, covered, for 4 hours or overnight. Drain cashews, rinse under cold water; drain well.

2 Lightly grease a 20cm x 30cm (8-inch x 12-inch) slice pan; line with plastic wrap, extending plastic 5cm (2-inches) over sides.

3 Process almonds, pecans, groats, desiccated coconut, cacao, coconut, mesquite, dates and ½ cup of the oil until coarse crumbs form and mixture starts to clump. Be careful not to over-process. Press nut mixture firmly and evenly over base of pan, using a spatula to form a 5mm (¼-inch) thick layer. Freeze for 15 minutes or until firm.

4 Lift biscuit base from pan; place on board. Cut base into 15 rounds using a 5cm (2-inch) cutter. Place rounds on a tray lined with baking paper; freeze while preparing peppermint cream.

5 To make peppermint cream, blend drained cashews with remaining coconut oil, coconut cream and agave syrup until as smooth as possible. Add extract; blend until combined. Pour peppermint cream into a small bowl; cover, freeze for 1 hour or until thick but not set, stirring occasionally.

6 Spoon 2 teaspoons of peppermint cream onto each biscuit round; using the back of the teaspoon, gently press down to flatten and smooth. Freeze for 3 hours or until set.

7 Make chocolate coating. Using a fork, lower biscuits, one at a time, into chocolate mixture. Allow excess chocolate to drain off, then place on tray. Refrigerate for 30 minutes or until chocolate is set.

chocolate coating Place coconut oil and cacao butter in a medium heatproof bowl over a smaller heatproof bowl of boiling water, whisk until combined and smooth; whisk in syrup. Whisk in cacao until combined and smooth. Pour into a small bowl.

TIPS Peppermint extract is available from health food stores. Buy peppermint extract rather than oil or essence, otherwise the flavour of the biscuits may be affected. Mesquite powder is available from some health food stores and gourmet food stores. If you have one, use a high-powered blender in step 5; this type of blender will produce a very smooth consistency.
DO-AHEAD Store biscuits in an airtight container in the fridge for up to 5 days.

Spiced easter buns with caramel butter

BUNS ARE BEST MADE ON DAY OF SERVING, HOWEVER, THEY CAN BE WARMED OR TOASTED THE NEXT DAY.

- **2 chai vanilla-flavoured tea bags**
- **¼ cup (60ml) boiling water**
- **1 tablespoon chia seeds**
- **1¼ cups (310ml) almond milk**
- **2 tablespoons pure maple syrup**
- **½ cup (125ml) olive oil**
- **2 teaspoons (7g) dry yeast**
- **5⅓ cups (800g) bread flour**
- **2 teaspoons mixed spice**
- **2 teaspoons salt**
- **¾ cup (120g) sultanas**
- **⅓ cup (40g) goji berries**
- **¼ cup (55g) crystallised ginger, chopped**
- **⅓ cup (50g) bread flour, extra**
- **¼ cup (60ml) water, extra**
- **1 teaspoon icing (confectioners') sugar**

CHAI GLAZE
- **½ cup (110g) caster (superfine) sugar**
- **⅓ cup (80ml) water**
- **1 chai vanilla-flavoured tea bag**

CARAMEL BUTTER
- **½ cup (125ml) pure maple syrup**
- **½ cup (140g) almond butter**
- **½ cup (110g) coconut oil, not melted (see tip)**
- **1 teaspoon vanilla extract**
- **1 teaspoon salt**

1 Place tea bags in a heatproof jug, pour over boiling water; stand for 5 minutes. Remove tea bags, squeezing out liquid; discard. Stir chia seeds into hot liquid with a fork; cool to room temperature.

2 Meanwhile, combine almond milk, syrup and oil in a medium jug; stir in yeast. Sift flour, spice and salt into a large bowl; stir in dried fruit and ginger. Add milk mixture and chia mixture; using your hands, mix together until well combined. Turn out onto a lightly floured surface; knead for 5 minutes.

3 Transfer dough to a lightly oiled bowl; cover. Stand in a warm place for 30 minutes.

4 Lightly knead dough for 10 seconds on a lightly oiled surface. Return dough to bowl; cover, stand in a warm place for 1 hour or until risen by half.

5 Divide dough into 24 pieces. Roll into balls; place on a large baking paper-lined tray in six rows. Cover; place in a warm place for 40 minutes or until risen by half.

6 Combine extra flour and the extra water with icing sugar in a small bowl to form a smooth paste. Spoon into a piping bag fitted with a 3mm (⅛-inch) tube. Pipe a cross pattern over buns.

7 Meanwhile, preheat oven to 200°C/400°F.

8 Bake buns for 25 minutes or until browned and the centre buns sound hollow when tapped.

9 Meanwhile, make chai glaze and caramel butter.

10 Brush hot buns with hot glaze. Serve warm or at room temperature with caramel butter.

chai glaze Stir ingredients in a small saucepan over medium heat until sugar dissolves; bring to the boil. Discard tea bag.

caramel butter Process ingredients until smooth. Refrigerate to thicken, if necessary.

TIP At cool room temperature, coconut oil will be solid. If liquid, refrigerate it to solidify before use.
SWAP You can used dried cranberries in place of goji berries.

Raw chocolate doughnuts with raspberry glaze

WE USED FREEZE-DRIED RASPBERRIES AND DESICCATED COCONUT TO DECORATE OUR DOUGHNUTS. YOU COULD ALSO USE SLIVERED NUTS OR EDIBLE DRIED ROSE PETALS.

- 1⅓ cups (300g) fresh dates, pitted
- ¾ cup (115g) raw cashews
- ¾ cup (120g) natural almonds
- ¾ cup (100g) hazelnuts
- ¾ cup (60g) desiccated coconut
- ⅓ cup (35g) cacao powder
- 2 tablespoons black chia seeds
- 2 tablespoons chocolate hazelnut butter
- desiccated coconut, extra, and freeze-dried raspberries, to serve

RASPBERRY GLAZE

- 1 cup (120g) frozen raspberries, thawed
- ⅓ cup (80g) melted coconut butter or paste (see tips)
- ⅓ cup (80ml) coconut cream
- 30g (1 ounce) coconut oil, melted
- 2 tablespoons coconut nectar
- 1 tablespoon lemon juice

1 Place dates in a small heatproof bowl; cover with hot water. Stand for 10 minutes. Drain dates; process until a smooth paste forms.

2 Process nuts until coarsely crushed. Add coconut, cacao powder, chia seeds, chocolate hazelnut butter and date paste; process until well combined and mixture starts to hold together.

3 Press mixture into silicon doughnut moulds or shape with hands (see tips). Place on a baking paper-lined tray; freeze for 30 minutes or until firm.

4 Meanwhile, make raspberry glaze.

5 Dip doughnuts into raspberry glaze; place on a wire rack over a tray to allow excess to drain away. Freeze for 10 minutes or until firm. Repeat dipping to double-coat doughnuts; freeze for 15 minutes. The glaze should be soft like a frosting. Smooth tops lightly with back of a teaspoon or a clean finger.

6 Serve doughnuts sprinkled with extra coconut and raspberries, if you like.

raspberry glaze Blend ingredients, including any raspberry juice, until as smooth as possible. Pour glaze into a small bowl.

TIPS Use a good-quality coconut butter that is creamy and not too dry. To melt coconut butter, place jar in a small bowl of boiling water; stand for 5 minutes, then stir to loosen.

If you have them, use silicone doughnut moulds; they create a perfect shape and doughnuts pop out with ease. If using doughnut pans, make sure to grease them. Otherwise, you can shape doughnuts by hand. Line a large oven tray with baking paper. Roll ¼-cups of the mixture into balls; flatten to around 2cm (¾-inch) high on the tray, then make hole in the centre. Shape with slightly damp hands into a more rounded shape.

DO-AHEAD Store doughnuts in an airtight container in the fridge for up to 5 days.

Raw Tiramisu

YOU CAN USE ESPRESSO, COLD-DRIP, PERCOLATOR OR PLUNGER COFFEE FOR THIS DELICIOUS RECIPE.

You will need to start this recipe a day ahead.

- **2 cups (300g) raw cashews**
- **1½ cups (120g) desiccated coconut**
- **¾ cup (75g) hazelnut meal**
- **½ cup (60g) almond meal**
- **¼ cup (20g) psyllium husks**
- **¼ cup (60ml) coconut milk**
- **¼ cup (60ml) coconut nectar**
- **½ teaspoon vanilla extract**
- **2 tablespoons espresso coffee**
- **2 teaspoons pure maple syrup**
- **¼ cup (25g) cacao powder**

COFFEE CREAM
- **½ cup (125ml) coconut cream**
- **¼ cup (60ml) pure maple syrup**
- **¼ cup (50g) coconut oil, melted**
- **⅓ cup (80ml) espresso coffee**
- **1 teaspoon pure vanilla extract**

VANILLA CREAM
- **¾ cup (180ml) coconut cream**
- **¼ cup (60ml) pure maple syrup**
- **¼ cup (50g) coconut oil, melted**
- **2 teaspoons vanilla extract**

1 Place cashews in a medium bowl; cover with cold water. Stand, covered, for 4 hours or overnight. Drain cashews, rinse under cold water; drain well. Reserve cashews for coffee cream and vanilla cream.

2 Lightly grease a 20cm x 30cm (8-inch x12-inch) slice pan; line base and long sides with baking paper, extending the paper 5cm (2 inches) over sides.

3 To make 'sponge', blend desiccated coconut until finely ground; transfer to a large bowl. Stir in nut meals and psyllium husks. Whisk coconut milk, nectar and vanilla in a small bowl. Add to dry ingredients; mix until well combined. Press sponge mixture evenly over base of pan. Refrigerate for 30 minutes to firm up slightly.

4 Meanwhile, whisk coffee and maple syrup in a small bowl until combined.

5 Make coffee cream.

6 Cut 12 x 6cm (2½-inch) rounds from sponge. Reserve and refrigerate 6 rounds. Dip 6 sponge pieces, one at a time, into coffee syrup and lightly press in base of six 1-cup (250ml) glasses or jars. Don't worry if the sponge breaks up.

7 Pour half the coffee cream over sponge bases; dust with sifted cacao powder. Freeze for 15 minutes to firm up slightly.

8 Make vanilla cream.

9 Pour half the vanilla cream over coffee cream layer; dust with sifted cacao powder. Freeze for 10 minutes to firm up slightly.

10 Repeat layering with reserved sponge rounds dipped in coffee syrup, coffee cream, sifted cacao powder, vanilla cream and sifted cacao powder, freezing between layers. Cover; refrigerate for 6 hours or until firm.

11 Dust with a little extra sifted cacao powder before serving.

coffee cream Blend half the cashews with all ingredients until as smooth as possible.

vanilla cream Blend remaining cashews with all ingredients until as smooth as possible.

TIP If you have one, use a high-powered blender in steps 5 and 8; this type of blender will produce a very smooth consistency. DO-AHEAD Store in a container in the fridge for up to 4 days.

Coconut & strawberry 'panna cotta'

THIS FRESH-FLAVOURED DESSERT ONLY HAS FOUR INGREDIENTS AND CAN BE MADE AHEAD OF TIME IF YOU ARE ENTERTAINING. SERVE IT IN GLASSES OR JARS.

- **4 young drinking coconuts (4kg)**
- **½ teaspoon agar agar powder (see tips)**
- **250g (8 ounces) fresh strawberries**
- **1 tablespoon lemon juice**
- **edible flowers, optional**

1 Place a coconut on its side on a chopping board; carefully cut off the dome-shaped top with a cleaver or large knife - you will need to use a bit of force. Drain coconut water into a large jug. Spoon out the soft flesh. Repeat with remaining coconuts; you should have about 2 cups (280g) of flesh.

2 Blend coconut flesh with 1 cup of the coconut water until as smooth as possible to form a puree.

3 Combine 1 cup of the coconut water (reserve leftover coconut water for another use) and agar agar in a small saucepan. Bring to a simmer, stirring, over low heat; simmer for 5 minutes. Add to coconut puree; blend until well combined.

4 Pour two-thirds of the coconut puree evenly into four 1-cup (250ml) glasses or jars. Refrigerate for 10 minutes or until set slightly.

5 Reserve half of the strawberries for serving; refrigerate. Hull remaining strawberries; add to remaining coconut puree with juice. Blend until as smooth as possible. Carefullly pour over set coconut mixture; refrigerate for 4 hours or until both layers are set.

6 Serve topped with reserved sliced or halved strawberries and edible flowers, if you like.

TIPS Agar agar is available from health food stores; it is a vegan substitute for gelatine, derived from seaweed.
If you have one, use a high-powered blender in steps 2, 3 and 5; this type of blender will produce a very smooth consistency.
DO-AHEAD Store 'panna cottas' in the fridge for up to 4 days.

Raw chocolate jaffa cake

IF YOU HAVE ONE, USE A HIGH-POWERED BLENDER; AS THIS WILL PRODUCE A VERY SMOOTH CONSISTENCY. YOU COULD ALSO BUY DEHYDRATED ORANGE SLICES.

You will need to start this recipe a day ahead.

- ¾ cup (120g) natural almonds
- ⅓ cup (40g) almond meal
- ¼ cup (25g) cacao powder
- ½ cup (100g) activated buckwheat groats
- ¼ cup (60ml) coconut nectar
- 20g (¾ ounce) coconut oil, melted
- ¾ teaspoon vanilla bean powder

CHOC-DIPPED ORANGE SLICES
- 1 medium orange (240g)
- 100g (3 ounces) vegan dark chocolate (70% cocoa), grated

FILLING
- 2 cups (300g) raw cashews
- ½ cup (125ml) pure maple syrup
- ½ cup (100g) coconut oil, melted
- ⅓ cup (35g) cacao powder
- 1½ tablespoons finely grated orange rind
- ¾ cup (180ml) fresh orange juice
- 40g (1½ ounces) cacao butter, melted
- ½ teaspoon vanilla bean powder

CHOCOLATE GANACHE
- ½ cup (50g) cacao powder
- ½ cup (125ml) pure maple syrup
- ¼ cup (50g) coconut oil, melted
- 1 teaspoon vanilla bean powder

1 Make choc-dipped orange slices and filling.

2 Grease a 23cm (9¼-inch) round springform cake pan. Line base and side with baking paper.

3 Process almonds, almond meal and cacao until mixture resembles coarse crumbs. Add buckwheat groats, coconut nectar, oil and vanilla; process until just combined. Press nut mixture firmly and evenly over base of pan using a spatula. Freeze for 15 minutes.

4 Pour filling over base; freeze for 2½ hours or until firm.

5 Make chocolate ganache. Pour over cake; smooth top. Refrigerate for 15 minutes or until set.

6 Remove cake from pan. Serve topped with choc-dipped orange slices; cut some in half, if you like.

choc-dipped orange slices Preheat dehydrator to 46°C/115°F. Cut orange into 3mm (⅛-inch) thick slices; remove any seeds. Arrange slices on mesh dehydrator trays. Dehydrate for 12-24 hours, turning slices halfway, or until slices are dry and brittle. Alternativley, preheat oven to its lowest temperature, ideally 50°C/122°F. Line an oven tray with baking paper, place a rectangular greased wire rack on top.

Arrange orange slices on rack. Place tray in oven; leave door slightly ajar so air can circulate and moisture can escape. Bake for 12 hours or until dry and brittle, turning slices occasionally. Melt chocolate in a small heatproof bowl over a bowl of hot water. Dip orange slices halfway into chocolate; gently shake away excess chocolate. Place slices on a tray lined with baking paper; refrigerate for 15 minutes or until set.

filling Place cashews in a medium bowl; cover with cold water. Stand, covered, for 4 hours or overnight. Drain cashews, rinse under cold water; drain well. Blend cashews with remaining ingredients until as smooth as possible.

chocolate ganache Blend ingredients until smooth and silky.

Raspberry cream slice

MESQUITE POWDER IS A NATIVE AMERICAN FOOD RICH IN MINERALS WITH A SWEET CARAMEL-LIKE TASTE; IT'S NOT CRITICAL TO THE RECIPE, SO OMIT IT IF YOU LIKE.

You will need to start this recipe a day ahead.

- **3 cups (450g) raw cashews**
- **3¾ cups (450g) frozen raspberries**
- **1 cup (140g) macadamias**
- **¾ cup (90g) pecans**
- **½ cup (40g) desiccated coconut**
- **7 fresh dates (140g), pitted**
- **1 teaspoon mesquite powder (see note above)**
- **¼ teaspoon salt**
- **⅔ cup (160ml) pure maple syrup**
- **⅓ cup (80ml) coconut cream**
- **1½ tablespoons finely grated lemon rind**
- **⅓ cup (80ml) lemon juice**
- **1 teaspoon vanilla bean powder**
- **½ cup (100g) coconut oil, melted**
- **40g (1½ ounces) cacao butter, melted**
- **2 tablespoons freeze-dried raspberries, optional**

1 Place cashews in a large bowl; cover with cold water. Stand, covered, for 4 hours or overnight. Drain cashews, rinse under cold water; drain well.
2 Thaw 3 cups of the raspberries in a medium bowl at room temperature for 1 hour.
3 Lightly grease an 18cm x 28cm (7¼-inch x 11¼-inch) slice pan; line base and sides with baking paper, extending paper 5cm (2 inches) over sides.
4 Process macadamias, pecans, desiccated coconut, dates, mesquite and salt until mixture resembles coarse crumbs and holds together when pressed. Press nut mixture firmly and evenly over base of pan, using a plastic spatula to form a 1cm (½-inch) thick layer. Refrigerate while preparing filling.
5 Blend drained cashews with syrup, coconut cream, rind, juice and vanilla until smooth. Slowly add coconut oil and cacao butter while motor is operating; blend until as smooth as possible. Add thawed raspberries, including any liquid; blend until well combined.
6 Pour one-third of raspberry mixture over biscuit base; smooth top. Scatter with remaining frozen raspberries; lightly press berries into filling. Pour over remaining raspberry mixture; smooth top. Cover; refrigerate overnight or until firm.
7 Cut slice into rectangles. Top with freeze-dried raspberries just before serving, if you like.

TIPS If you have one, use a high-speed blender in step 5; this type of blender will produce a very smooth consistency. Mesquite powder and cacao butter are available from some health food stores and gourmet food stores. Freeze-dried raspberries are available from some health food stores, chef's suppliers and gourmet food stores; they can also be purchased online.
DO-AHEAD Store in an airtight container in the fridge for up to 5 days. Undecorated slice can be frozen in a container for up to 2 months. Slice is best eaten within 30 minutes of removing from freezer.

Raw choc–peanut cake

THE CAKE KEEPS IN AN AIRTIGHT CONTAINER IN THE FRIDGE FOR UP TO 5 DAYS OR FROZEN FOR 2 MONTHS.

Start this recipe a day ahead. Use a high-powered blender, if possible.

- ½ cup (80g) natural almonds
- ¾ cup (90g) almond meal
- ¾ cup (60g) desiccated coconut
- ¼ cup (60ml) pure maple syrup
- 2 tablespoons almond butter
- ⅓ cup (40g) cacao powder
- ¼ teaspoon vanilla bean powder
- 1 cup (140g) roasted unsalted peanuts, chopped coarsely

NOUGAT

- 2½ cups (375g) raw cashews
- 1 cup (250ml) coconut cream
- ½ cup (125ml) pure maple syrup
- ½ cup (130g) almond butter
- 1 cup (80g) desiccated coconut
- ½ cup (100g) coconut oil, melted
- 2 teaspoons mesquite powder
- ½ teaspoon vanilla bean powder

CARAMEL

- 1 cup (140g) fresh dates, pitted
- ½ cup (140g) smooth peanut butter
- ¼ cup (60ml) coconut cream
- ¼ cup (50g) coconut oil, melted
- 1 tablespoon pure maple syrup
- 2 teaspoons mesquite powder
- ¼ teaspoon salt

CHOCOLATE TOPPING

- ¼ cup (50g) coconut oil
- ¼ cup (60g) cacao butter, chopped
- ¼ cup (60ml) pure maple syrup
- ⅔ cup (70g) cacao powder

1 Make nougat.

2 Grease a 23cm (9¼-inch) round springform cake pan. Line base and side with baking paper.

3 Process almonds until coarsely chopped. Add almond meal, coconut, syrup, almond butter, 2 tablespoons of the cacao powder and vanilla powder; process until combined and mixture starts to stick together. Press mixture over base of pan; smooth surface with a plastic spatula. Freeze until required.

4 Pour two-thirds of the nougat over base; freeze for 30 minutes.

5 Add remaining cacao powder to the remaining nougat mixture; blend until well combined. Spread over nougat layer; smooth top. Freeze for 3 hours or until firm.

6 Make caramel. Spread caramel over cake; sprinkle with chopped peanuts. Freeze for 30 minutes or until caramel firms up slightly.

7 Make chocolate topping.

8 Remove cake from pan; place on a plate. Drizzle chocolate topping over cake, allowing it to drip down the sides. Using a palette knife, smooth chocolate on top of cake. Refrigerate for 30 minutes or until set.

nougat Place cashews in a medium bowl; cover with cold water. Stand, covered, for 4 hours or overnight. Drain cashews, rinse under cold water; drain well. Blend drained cashews with coconut cream, syrup and almond butter until as smooth as possible. Add remaining ingredients; blend until well combined.

caramel Place dates in a small bowl; just cover with cold water. Stand for 30 minutes, drain. Blend drained dates with remaining ingredients until as smooth as possible.

chocolate topping Place coconut oil and cacao butter in a medium heatproof bowl over a smaller heatproof bowl of boiling water, whisk until combined and smooth; whisk in syrup. Whisk in cacao until combined and smooth.

SERVING IDEAS Scatter peanuts over the top before serving or drizzle with melted vegan salted caramel chocolate.

Strawberry mylkshake popsicles

PERFECT FOR A SWELTERING SUMMER'S DAY, THESE LUSCIOUS POPS ARE BEST MADE WITH STRAWBERRIES AT THEIR RIPEST, WITH A STRONG AROMA AND TASTE.

You will need to start this recipe a day ahead.

- ¼ cup (40g) raw cashews
- 1⅔ cups (400ml) coconut cream
- ¼ cup (60ml) pure maple syrup
- 1 teaspoon pure vanilla extract
- 200g (6½ ounces) strawberries, hulled

CHOCOLATE COATING

- ¼ cup (50g) coconut oil
- ¼ cup (60g) cacao butter, chopped
- 2 tablespoons pure maple syrup
- ½ cup (50g) cacao powder

1 Place cashews in a medium bowl; cover with cold water. Stand, covered, for 4 hours or overnight. Drain cashews, rinse under cold water; drain well.
2 Blend drained cashews with coconut cream, syrup, vanilla and strawberries until as smooth as possible.
3 Pour mixture into eight ⅓-cup (80ml) popsicle moulds; freeze for 1 hour. Insert popsicle sticks; freeze overnight or until firm.
4 Run moulds quickly under cold water; remove popsicles. Place popsicles on a tray lined with baking paper; return tray to freezer.
5 Make chocolate coating.
6 Dip tip of popsicles, one at a time, into chocolate coating. Gently shake off excess chocolate. Return to lined tray; freeze for 5 minutes or until chocolate is firm. If you want to alternate the chocolate pattern, drizzle some of the popsicles with chocolate (see tips).

chocolate coating Place coconut oil and cacao butter in a medium heatproof bowl over a smaller heatproof bowl of boiling water, whisk until combined and smooth; whisk in syrup. Whisk in cacao until combined and smooth. Pour chocolate into a small wide glass; this will make it easier to dip the popsicles.

TIPS To create thin drizzled lines of chocolate on the popsicles, use a plastic snap-lock bag. Spoon melted vegan chocolate into the bag, then cut off a tiny tip on one corner of the bag. Drizzle chocolate over popsicles. Freeze for 5 minutes or until set; turn over and repeat.
If you have one, use a high-speed blender in step 2; this type of blender will produce a very smooth consistency.
DO-AHEAD Store popsicles in an airtight container, placing a sheet of baking paper between them. Popsicles can be frozen for up to 2 months.

Raw strawberry & cream cheesecake

THE CAKE WILL KEEP IN AN AIRTIGHT CONTAINER IN THE FRIDGE FOR UP TO 4 DAYS. IF YOU HAVE ONE, USE A HIGH-POWERED BLENDER FOR SMOOTH RESULTS.

You will need to start this recipe 2 days ahead.

- 2½ cups (375g) raw cashews
- 1 cup (140g) macadamias
- ¾ cup (60g) desiccated coconut
- ½ cup (60g) almond meal
- 6 fresh dates (120g), pitted
- ¾ teaspoon vanilla bean powder
- ¾ cup (150g) coconut oil, melted
- 400g (12½ ounces) small strawberries
- 1 cup (240g) vegan coconut yoghurt
- ½ cup (125ml) light agave syrup
- 1 tablespoon finely grated lemon rind
- ⅓ cup (80ml) lemon juice
- ⅓ cup (80g) cacao butter, melted

1 Place cashews in a medium bowl; cover with cold water. Stand, covered, for 4 hours or overnight. Drain cashews, rinse under cold water; drain well.

2 Grease a 23cm (9¼-inch) round springform cake pan. Line base and side of pan with baking paper, extending paper 5cm (2 inches) above edge of pan.

3 Process macadamias, desiccated coconut, almond meal, dates and ¼ teaspoon of the vanilla powder until mixture resembles coarse crumbs. Add 1 tablespoon oil; process until combined and mixture starts to stick together. Press mixture over base of pan; use the back of a spoon to press down firmly and smooth surface.

4 Thinly slice a quarter of the strawberries lengthways. Strawberries shouldn't be more than 3.5cm (1½ inches) long, or the tips won't be covered by filling; trim strawberries if needed. Arrange strawberry slices around side of cake pan, sticking them to the baking paper. Refrigerate cake pan until required.

5 Blend drained cashews, yoghurt, syrup, rind, juice and remaining vanilla powder until as smooth as possible. Add cacao butter and remaining oil; blend until as smooth as possible. Pour two-thirds of the mixture over base; smooth top. Refrigerate while preparing strawberry layer.

6 Hull remaining strawberries; add to remaining mixture, blend until as smooth as possible. Gently spoon strawberry mixture over cream layer; do not pour or layers will combine.

7 Refrigerate cake overnight or until set. For best results, allow cake to set in fridge for 18 hours before serving.

8 Remove cake from pan and place on a plate to serve.

SERVING IDEAS Serve topped with unsprayed roses or other flowers, raspberries dusted in icing sugar, extra halved strawberries and heart-shaped chocolates, if you like.

PREP + COOK TIME 30 MINUTES
MAKES 1 LITRE (4 CUPS)

Dulce de leche

OUR VERSION OF THE SOUTH
AMERICAN CARAMEL SAUCE USES
COCONUT CREAM TO MAKE A
DECADENT VEGAN ALTERNATIVE.
USE AS A TOPPING FOR VEGAN
ICE-CREAM, BLENDED WITH NUT
MILK (PAGE 28) FOR A CARAMEL
MILKSHAKE OR DRIZZLED OVER
OUR BANOFFEE PIE (PAGE 186).

Combine 800ml coconut cream and 4 cups (640g)
coconut sugar in a medium saucepan over medium heat.
Stir until sugar dissolves; bring to a simmer. Simmer,
stirring frequently, for 20 minutes or until it thickens to
a caramel consistency. Pour into sterilised jars; seal.
Cool. Refrigerate for up to 2 weeks.

TIP For information on how to sterilise jars, see glossary,
page 283.

popcorn dulce de leche Make dulce de leche; cool slightly.
Stir in 1 cup (15g) coarsely chopped salted popcorn.

orange & hazelnut dulce de leche Make dulce de leche.
While still warm, stir in 2 teaspoons finely grated orange
rind and ½ cup (70g) coarsely chopped roasted hazelnuts.

Caramelised banana choc-tops

VEGAN WAFFLE CONES CAN BE PURCHASED FROM MOST HEALTH FOOD STORES AND LARGE SUPERMARKETS – CHECK INGREDIENTS ON PACKAGING TO BE SURE.

You will need to start this recipe a day ahead.

- ½ cup (75g) raw cashews
- 2 medium ripe bananas (400g)
- ½ cup (125ml) pure maple syrup
- 1⅔ cups (400ml) coconut cream
- 2 teaspoons pure vanilla extract
- 2 tablespoons cacao nibs
- 6 vegan waffle cones (see note above)

CHOCOLATE TOPPING

- 80g (2½ ounces) coconut oil
- ¼ cup (60g) cacao butter, chopped
- 2 tablespoons pure maple syrup
- ½ cup (50g) cacao powder

1 Place cashews in a medium bowl; cover with cold water. Stand, covered, for 4 hours or overnight. Drain cashews, rinse under cold water; drain well.

2 Preheat oven to 180°C/350°F.

3 Slice bananas; place on an oven tray. Drizzle with ¼ cup of the syrup; toss to coat. Bake for 25 minutes or until caramelised.

4 Blend caramelised bananas with drained cashews, remaining syrup, coconut cream and vanilla until as smooth as possible. Stir in cacao nibs. Pour mixture into a 1-litre (4-cup) freezerproof container. Cover; freeze overnight or until firm.

5 Stand frozen banana mixture for 15 minutes to soften slightly. Scoop banana mixture; place into cones. Place cones in tall glasses or a cone stand; freeze for 20 minutes or until firm.

6 Meanwhile, make chocolate topping.

7 Dip ice-cream cones, one at a time, in chocolate topping. Return to freezer for 10 minutes or until chocolate is set. Cones are best eaten immediately.

chocolate topping Place coconut oil and cacao butter in a medium heatproof bowl over a smaller heatproof bowl of boiling water, whisk until combined and smooth; whisk in syrup. Whisk in cacao until combined and smooth. Pour chocolate into a small deep bowl; this will make it easier to dip the ice-creams.

TIPS If you have one, use a high-powered blender in step 4; this type of blender will produce a very smooth consistency.
DO AHEAD Ice-cream will keep in freezer for up to 2 months.

Raw coconut lime cake

DECORATE CAKE WITH SHAVED FRESH COCONUT AND THINLY SLICED LIME RIND OR SLICED MANGO DRESSED IN LIME JUICE WHEN IT IS IN SEASON

- 2½ cups (200g) desiccated coconut
- ⅔ cup (140g) coconut oil, melted
- ⅔ cup (160ml) rice malt syrup
- ⅓ cup (80ml) coconut cream
- 40g (1½ ounces) coconut butter, melted
- 4 young drinking coconuts (4kg)
- ¼ cup (60ml) lime juice

LIME SYRUP
- 2 medium limes (180g)
- ½ cup (125ml) coconut nectar

1 Grease a 20cm (8-inch) round springform cake pan. Line base and sides with baking paper.

2 Process 1 cup of the desiccated coconut until finely ground; transfer to a large bowl. Add ½ cup of the remaining desiccated coconut and 1 tablespoon each of the oil, syrup, coconut cream and coconut butter; mix until well combined. Lightly press mixture into pan; smooth surface with a plastic spatula. Freeze for 15 minutes or until firm.

3 Meanwhile, place a coconut on its side on a chopping board; carefully cut off the dome-shaped top with a cleaver or large knife – you will need to use a bit of force. Drain coconut water into a large jug; keep for another use. Spoon out the soft flesh. Repeat with remaining coconuts; you should have about 2½ cups of flesh.

4 Blend coconut flesh and lime juice with remaining oil and syrup until as smooth as possible. Add remaining desiccated coconut, coconut cream and coconut butter; blend until well combined. Pour mixture over base; smooth top. Freeze for 4 hours or until firm.

5 Meanwhile, make lime syrup.

6 Remove cake from pan; place on a plate. Serve with lime syrup.

lime syrup Remove rind from limes using a zester. (Or, peel rind thinly from limes, avoiding white pith. Cut rind into long thin strips.) Squeeze ¼ cup of juice from limes. Combine zest, juice and nectar in a small saucepan; bring to the boil. Reduce heat; simmer, uncovered, for 2 minutes or until thickened.

TIP If you have one, use a high-powered blender in step 4; this type of blender will produce a very smooth consistency. **DO-AHEAD** Store cake in an airtight container in the fridge for up to 5 days. The undecorated cake can be frozen in a container for up to 2 months. Cake is best eaten within 45 minutes of removing from freezer.

Choc-coated nutty dates

IF YOU AVOID DAIRY PRODUCTS FOR ALLERGY REASONS, APPROACH DARK CHOCOLATE WITH CAUTION, AS EVEN THOSE LABELLED VEGAN OR DAIRY-FREE MAY NOT BE.

- **100g (3 ounces) vegan dark chocolate (70% cocoa), chopped**
- **10 fresh dates (200g), pitted**
- **5 teaspoons super seed spread or nut butter**
- **10 pecans**
- **¼ teaspoon sea salt flakes**

1 Place chocolate in a small heatproof bowl; stir over a small saucepan of simmering water until smooth (don't let water touch base of bowl).

2 Line an oven tray with baking paper. Cut a slit in the top of each date. Fill each date with ½ teaspoon spread and 1 pecan. Press date to enclose filling.

3 Dip dates in melted chocolate to coat; place on prepared tray. Sprinkle with salt. Stand in a cool place until chocolate is set.

SWAP Use any combination of nut butter and nuts.

DO-AHEAD If making ahead of time, store in an airtight container in the fridge.

Glossary

ACTIVATED BUCKINIS made with buckwheat, which, despite its name, is not actually a wheat, but is a fruit belonging to the same family as rhubarb. It's gluten free, high in protein and essential amino acids, and is a rich source of minerals and B vitamins.

AGAVE SYRUP from the agave plant; has a low GI, but that is due to the high percentage of fructose present, which may be harmful in large quantities.

ALLSPICE also called pimento or jamaican pepper; tastes like a combination of nutmeg, cumin, clove and cinnamon. Available whole or ground.

ALMONDS
flat, pointy-tipped nuts with a pitted brown shell enclosing a creamy white kernel which is covered by a brown skin.

blanched brown skins removed.

flaked paper-thin slices.

meal nuts are powdered to a coarse flour-like texture.

slivered small pieces cut lengthways.

ARROWROOT a starch made from the rhizome of a Central American plant, used mostly as a thickening agent.

BAKING POWDER a raising agent consisting mainly of two parts cream of tartar to one part bicarbonate of soda. see also gluten-free baking powder.

BARLEY a nutritious grain used in soups and stews. Hulled barley, the least processed, is high in fibre. Pearl barley has had the husk removed then been steamed and polished so that only the 'pearl' of the original grain remains, much the same as white rice.

BAY LEAVES aromatic leaves from the bay tree available fresh or dried; adds a strong, slightly peppery flavour.

BEANS
black also called turtle beans or black kidney beans; an earthy-flavoured dried bean completely different from the better-known Chinese black beans (fermented soybeans). Used mostly in Mexican and South American cooking.

borlotti also called roman beans or pink beans, can be eaten fresh or dried. Interchangeable with pinto beans due to their similarity in appearance – pale pink or beige with dark red streaks.

cannellini small white bean similar in appearance and flavour to other phaseolus vulgaris varieties (great northern, navy or haricot). Available dried or canned.

green also known as french or string beans (although the tough string they once had has generally been bred out of them), this long thin fresh bean is consumed in its entirety once cooked.

soy the most nutritious of all legumes; high in protein and low in carbohydrate and the source of products such as tofu, soy milk, soy sauce, tamari and miso. Sometimes sold fresh as edamame; also available dried and canned.

sprouts tender new growths of assorted beans and seeds germinated for consumption as sprouts.

BICARBONATE OF SODA (baking soda) a raising agent.

BUCKWHEAT a herb in the same plant family as rhubarb; not a cereal so it is gluten-free. Available as flour; ground (cracked) into coarse, medium or fine granules (kasha) and used similarly to polenta; or groats, the whole kernel sold roasted as a cereal product.

CACAO
butter is rich in saturated fats; about a third is stearic acid, but this acts differently to other saturated fats in that it doesn't raise cholesterol and, in fact, lowers LDL (bad) cholesterol. It is available from some health food stores and gourmet food stores.

nibs can be separated into cocoa butter and powder. Cocoa powder retains many beneficial antioxidants and is an easy way of adding cocoa into your diet without the kilojoules of chocolate.

powder is made by removing the cocoa butter using a process known as cold-pressing. It retains more of its nutrients than heat-processed cacao powder; it also has a stronger, slightly bitter, taste.

CASHEWS plump, kidney-shaped, golden-brown nuts having a distinctive sweet, buttery flavour and containing about 48% fat. Because of this high fat content, they should be kept, sealed tightly, under refrigeration to avoid becoming rancid. We use roasted unsalted cashews in this book, unless otherwise stated; they're available from health-food stores and most supermarkets. Roasting cashews brings out their intense nutty flavour.

CHIA SEEDS contain protein and all the essential amino acids and a wealth of vitamins, minerals and antioxidants, as well as being fibre-rich.

CHICKPEAS (garbanzo beans) also called hummus or channa; an irregularly round, sandy-coloured legume used extensively in Mediterranean, Indian and Hispanic cooking. Firm texture even after cooking, a floury mouth-feel and robust nutty flavour; available canned or dried (reconstitute for several hours in cold water before use).

CHILLI available in many different types and sizes. Use rubber gloves when seeding and chopping fresh chillies as they can burn your skin. Removing seeds and membranes lessens the heat level.

chipotle pronounced cheh-pote-lay. The name used for jalapeño chillies once they've been dried and smoked. Having a deep, intensely smokey flavour, rather than a searing heat, chipotles are dark brown, almost black in colour and wrinkled in appearance.

flakes also sold as crushed chilli; dehydrated deep-red extremely fine slices and whole seeds.

green any unripened chilli; also some particular varieties that are ripe when green, such as jalapeño, habanero, poblano or serrano.

jalapeño pronounced hah-lah-pain-yo. Fairly hot, medium-sized, plump, dark green chilli; available pickled, sold canned or bottled, and fresh, from greengrocers.

long red available both fresh and dried; a generic term used for any moderately hot, long, thin chilli (about 6cm to 8cm long).

COCONUT

cream comes from the first pressing of the coconut flesh, without the addition of water; the second pressing (less rich) is sold as coconut milk. Look for coconut cream labelled as 100% coconut, without added emulsifiers.

desiccated concentrated, dried, unsweetened and finely shredded coconut flesh.

flaked dried flaked coconut flesh.

milk not the liquid found inside the fruit (coconut water), but the diluted liquid from the second pressing of the white flesh of a mature coconut (the first pressing produces coconut cream).

oil is extracted from the coconut flesh so you don't get any of the fibre, protein or carbohydrates present in the whole coconut. The best quality is virgin coconut oil, which is the oil pressed from the dried coconut flesh, and doesn't include the use of solvents or other refining processes.

shredded thin strips of dried coconut.

sugar is not made from coconuts, but from the sap of the blossoms of the coconut palm tree. The refined sap looks a little like raw or light brown sugar, and has a similar caramel flavour. It also has the same amount of kilojoules as regular table (white) sugar.

water is the liquid from the centre of a young green coconut. It has fewer kilojoules than fruit juice, with no fat or protein. There are sugars present, but these are slowly absorbed giving coconut water a low GI.

young are coconuts that are not fully mature. As a coconut ages, the amount of juice inside decreases, until it eventually disappears and is replaced by air.

CORIANDER (cilantro) also known as pak chee or chinese parsley; a bright-green leafy herb with a pungent flavour. Both stems and roots of coriander are also used in cooking; wash well before using. Also available ground or as seeds; these should not be substituted for fresh.

CORNFLOUR (cornstarch) available made from corn or wheat (wheaten cornflour, which contains gluten, gives a lighter texture in cakes); used as a thickening agent in cooking.

CUMIN also known as zeera or comino; resembling a caraway in size, cumin is the dried seed of a plant related to the parsley family and has a spicy, nutty flavour. Available in seed form or dried and ground.

DATES fruit of the date palm tree, eaten fresh or dried, on their own or in dishes. About 4-6cm (1½-2¼ inches) in length, oval and plump, thin-skinned, with a honey-sweet flavour and sticky texture.

EDAMAME (shelled soy beans) available frozen from Asian food stores and some supermarkets.

EGGPLANT also called aubergine. Ranging in size from tiny to very large and in colour from pale green to deep purple.

FENNEL a roundish, bulbous vegetable, about 8-12cm in diameter, with a mild licorice smell and taste. The bulb has a slightly sweet, anise flavour but the leaves have a much stronger taste. Also the name given to dried seeds having a licorice flavour.

FLOUR

chickpea (besan) creamy yellow flour made from chickpeas and is very nutritious.

plain (all-purpose) a general all-purpose wheat flour.

rice very fine, almost powdery, gluten-free flour; made from ground white rice. Used in baking, as a thickener, and in some Asian noodles and desserts.

self-raising plain flour sifted with baking powder in the proportion of 1 cup flour to 2 teaspoons baking powder.

tapioca made from the root of the cassava plant; a soft, fine, light white flour.

wholemeal also known as wholewheat flour; milled with the wheat germ so is higher in fibre and more nutritional than plain flour.

FREEKEH is cracked roasted green wheat and can be found in some larger supermarkets, health food and specialty food stores.

GARAM MASALA a blend of spices that includes cardamom, cloves, cumin, cinnamon, coriander, and fennel . Black pepper and chilli can also be added for heat.

GAI LAN also known as gai larn, chinese broccoli and chinese kale; green vegetable appreciated more for its stems than its coarse leaves. Can be served steamed and stir-fried, in soups and noodle dishes.

GINGER

crystallised also called candied ginger. Fresh ginger root preserved in sugar syrup.

fresh also called green or root ginger; the thick gnarled root of a tropical plant. Can be kept, peeled, covered with dry sherry in a jar and refrigerated, or frozen in an airtight container.

ground also called powdered ginger; used as a flavouring in baking but cannot be substituted for fresh ginger.

pickled pink or red coloured; available, packaged, from Asian food shops. Pickled paper-thin shavings of ginger in a mixture of vinegar, sugar and natural colouring; used in Japanese cooking.

GOJI BERRIES (dried) small, very juicy, sweet red berries that grow on a type of shrub in Tibet. Believed to be high in nutrients and antioxidants.

HARISSA a Moroccan paste made from dried chillies, cumin, garlic, oil and caraway seeds. Available from Middle Eastern food shops and supermarkets.

HAZELNUTS also known as filberts; plump, grape-sized, rich, sweet nut having a brown skin that is removed by rubbing heated nuts together vigorously in a tea-towel.

meal is made by grounding the hazelnuts to a coarse flour texture for use in baking or as a thickening agent.

LEEKS a member of the onion family, the leek resembles a green onion but is much larger and more subtle in flavour. Tender baby or pencil leeks can be eaten whole with minimal cooking but adult leeks are usually trimmed of most of the green tops then sliced.

LEMON GRASS also known as takrai, serai or serah. A tall, clumping, lemon-smelling and tasting, sharp-edged aromatic tropical grass; the white lower part of the stem is used, finely chopped, in much of the cooking of South-East Asia.

LENTILS (red, brown, yellow) dried pulses often identified by and named after their colour. Eaten by cultures all over the world, most famously perhaps in the dhals of India.

French-style a local cousin to the famous (and very expensive) French lentils du puy; green-blue, tiny lentils with a nutty, earthy flavour and a hardy nature that allows them to be rapidly cooked without disintegrating.

LINSEEDS also known as flaxseeds, they are the richest plant source of omega 3 fats, which are essential for a healthy brain, heart, joints and immune system.

MACADAMIAS native to Australia; fairly large, slightly soft, buttery rich nut. Used to make oil and macadamia butter; equally good in salads or cakes and pastries; delicious eaten on their own.

MAPLE SYRUP also called pure maple syrup; distilled from the sap of sugar maple trees found only in Canada and the USA. Maple-flavoured syrup or pancake syrup is not an adequate substitute for the real thing.

MATCHA finely ground green tea powder. Matcha is rich in antioxidants called polyphenols, which have been linked to prevention against heart disease and cancer. Made from the whole ground tea leaf, matcha contains three times the amount of caffeine than in a cup of steeped tea, instead being comparable to that of a cup of coffee.

MILLET is a small-seeded cereal grain, which has a slightly nutty, corn-like flavour. Puffed millet are grains that have been processed under high pressure with steam, causing them to expand and puff; it is available from health food stores and the health food section of large supermarkets.

MISO fermented soybean paste. There are many types of miso, each with its own aroma, flavour, colour and texture; it can be kept, airtight, for up to a year in the fridge. Buy in tubs or plastic packs.

MUSHROOMS

button small, cultivated white mushrooms with a mild flavour. When a recipe in this book calls for an unspecified type of mushroom, use button.

enoki also known as enokitake, also enokidake; is a long, thin white mushroom used in East Asian cuisine.

oyster also known as abalone; grey-white mushrooms shaped like a fan. Prized for their smooth texture and subtle, oyster-like flavour.

portobello are mature, fully opened swiss browns; they are larger and bigger in flavour.

shiitake are also known as Chinese black, forest or golden oak mushrooms. Although cultivated, they have the earthiness and taste of wild mushrooms. swiss brown also known as cremini or roman mushrooms; are light brown mushrooms with a full-bodied flavour.

NORI a type of dried seaweed used in Japanese cooking as a flavouring, garnish or for sushi. Sold in thin sheets, plain or toasted (yaki-nori).

NUTMEG a strong and pungent spice ground from the dried nut of an evergreen tree native to Indonesia. Usually found ground but the flavour is more intense from a whole nut, available from spice shops, so it's best to grate your own. Used most often in baking and milk-based desserts, but also works nicely in savoury dishes. Found in mixed spice mixtures.

OIL

coconut see *Coconut*

olive made from ripened olives. Extra virgin and virgin are the first and second press, respectively, of the olives; "light" refers to taste not fat levels.

peanut pressed from ground peanuts; most commonly used oil in Asian cooking because of its high smoke point (capacity to handle high heat without burning).

rice bran is extracted from the germ and inner husk of the rice grain; has a mild, slightly nutty, flavour. Its high smoke point means it's suitable for high-temperature cooking methods such as stir frying and deep frying.

sesame used as a flavouring rather than a cooking medium.

vegetable oils sourced from plant rather than animal fats.

ONIONS

green (scallions) also called, incorrectly, shallot; an immature onion picked before the bulb has formed, has a long, bright-green stalk.

red also known as spanish, red spanish or bermuda onion; a sweet-flavoured, large, purple-red onion.

shallots also called french or golden shallots or eschalots; small and brown-skinned.

POLENTA also known as cornmeal; a flour-like cereal made of ground corn (maize). Also the name of the dish made from it.

POMEGRANATE dark-red, leathery-skinned fruit about the size of an orange filled with hundreds of seeds, each wrapped in an edible lucent-crimson pulp with a unique tangy sweet-sour flavour.

QUINOA is the seed of a leafy plant similar to spinach. It has a delicate, slightly nutty taste and chewy texture.

flakes the grains have been rolled and flattened.

puffed has been steamed until it puffs up.

RICE MALT SYRUP also known as brown rice syrup or rice syrup; is made by cooking brown rice flour with enzymes to break down its starch into sugars from which the water is removed.

ROASTING/TOASTING desiccated coconut, pine nuts and sesame seeds roast more evenly if stirred over low heat in a heavy-based frying pan; their natural oils will help turn them golden brown. Remove from pan immediately. Nuts and dried coconut can be roasted in the oven to release their aromatic essential oils. Spread them evenly onto an oven tray then roast at 180°C/350°F for about 5 minutes.

SEMOLINA coarsely ground flour milled from durum wheat; the flour used in making gnocchi, pasta and couscous.

SESAME SEEDS black and white are the most common of this small oval seed, however there are also red and brown varieties. The seeds are used as an ingredient and as a condiment. Roast the seeds in a heavy-based frying pan over low heat.

STERLISING JARS

It's important the jars be as clean as possible; make sure your hands, the preparation area, tea towels and cloths etc, are clean, too. The aim is to finish sterilising the jars and lids at the same time the preserve is ready to be bottled; the hot preserve should be bottled into hot, dry clean jars. Jars that aren't sterilised properly can cause deterioration of the preserves during storage. Always start with cleaned washed jars and lids, then follow one of these methods:

(1) Put jars and lids through the hottest cycle of a dishwasher without using any detergent.

(2) Lie jars down in a boiler with the lids, cover them with cold water then cover the boiler with a lid. Bring the water to the boil over a high heat and boil the jars for 20 minutes.

(3) Stand jars upright, without touching each other, on a wooden board on the lowest shelf in the oven. Turn the oven to the lowest possible temperature; leave jars to heat for 30 minutes.

Remove the jars from the oven or dishwasher with a towel, or from the boiling water with tongs and rubber-gloved hands; the water will evaporate from hot wet jars quite quickly. Stand jars upright and not touching on a wooden board, or a bench covered with a towel to protect and insulate the bench. Fill the jars as directed in the recipe; secure the lids tightly, holding jars firmly with a towel or an oven mitt. Leave at room temperature to cool before storing.

SUGAR

brown very soft, finely granulated sugar retaining molasses for its characteristic colour and flavour.

caster (superfine) finely granulated table sugar.

coconut see Coconut

palm also called nam tan pip, jaggery, jawa or gula melaka; made from the sap of the sugar palm tree. Light brown to black in colour and usually sold in rock-hard cakes; use brown sugar if unavailable.

pure icing (confectioners') also known as powdered sugar.

raw natural brown granulated sugar.

TAHINI a rich, sesame-seed paste, used in most Middle-Eastern cuisines, especially Lebanese, in dips and sauces.

TAMARI a thick, dark soy sauce made mainly from soya beans, but without the wheat used in most standard soy sauces.

TEMPEH a traditional soy product originating from Indonesia. It is made by a natural culturing and controlled fermentation process that binds soybeans into a cake form.

TOFU also called bean curd; an off-white, custard-like product made from the "milk" of crushed soybeans. Comes fresh as soft or firm, and processed as fried or pressed dried sheets. Fresh tofu can be refrigerated in water (changed daily) for up to 4 days.

firm made by compressing bean curd to remove most of the water. Good used in stir-fries as it can be tossed without disintegrating. Can also be flavoured, preserved in rice wine or brine.

silken not a type of tofu but reference to the manufacturing process of straining soybean liquid through silk; this denotes best quality.

TURMERIC also called kamin; is a rhizome related to galangal and ginger. Must be grated or pounded to release its acrid aroma and pungent flavour. Known for the golden colour it imparts, fresh turmeric can be substituted with the more commonly found dried powder. When fresh turmeric is called for in a recipe, the dried powder can be substituted (proportions are 1 teaspoon of ground turmeric for every 20g of fresh turmeric).

VANILLA

bean dried, long, thin pod from a tropical golden orchid; the minuscule black seeds inside the bean impart a luscious flavour in baking and desserts.

extract obtained from vanilla beans infused in water; a non-alcoholic version of essence.

paste made from vanilla beans and contains real seeds. Is highly concentrated: 1 teaspoon replaces a whole vanilla bean. Found in most supermarkets in the baking section.

VINEGAR

balsamic made from the juice of Trebbiano grapes; it is a deep rich brown colour with a sweet and sour flavour.

cider made from fermented apples.

rice wine made from rice wine lees (sediment left after fermentation), salt and alcohol.

wine based on red wine.

WASABI also called wasabe; an Asian horseradish used to make the pungent, green-coloured sauce traditionally served with Japanese raw fish dishes; sold in powdered or paste form.

XANTHAN GUM is a thickening agent produced by fermentation of, usually, corn sugar. When buying xanthan gum, ensure the packet states 'made from fermented corn sugar'. Found in the health-food section in larger supermarkets.

YEAST (dried and fresh), a raising agent used in dough making. Granular (7g sachets) and fresh compressed (20g blocks) yeast can almost always be substituted for the other.

ZA'ATAR a blend of whole roasted sesame seeds, sumac and crushed dried herbs such as wild marjoram and thyme, its content is largely determined by the individual maker. Used to flavour many familiar Middle Eastern dishes, pizza and savoury pastries..

Conversion chart

MEASURES

One Australian metric measuring cup holds approximately 250ml; one Australian metric tablespoon holds 20ml; one Australian metric teaspoon holds 5ml.

The difference between one country's measuring cups and another's is within a two- or three-teaspoon variance, and will not affect your cooking results. North America, New Zealand and the United Kingdom use a 15ml tablespoon.

All cup and spoon measurements are level. The most accurate way of measuring dry ingredients is to weigh them. When measuring liquids, use a clear glass or plastic jug with the metric markings.
We use large eggs with an average weight of 60g.

DRY MEASURES

metric	imperial
15g	½oz
30g	1oz
60g	2oz
90g	3oz
125g	4oz (¼lb)
155g	5oz
185g	6oz
220g	7oz
250g	8oz (½lb)
280g	9oz
315g	10oz
345g	11oz
375g	12oz (¾lb)
410g	13oz
440g	14oz
470g	15oz
500g	16oz (1lb)
750g	24oz (1½lb)
1kg	32oz (2lb)

LIQUID MEASURES

metric	imperial
30ml	1 fluid oz
60ml	2 fluid oz
100ml	3 fluid oz
125ml	4 fluid oz
150ml	5 fluid oz
190ml	6 fluid oz
250ml	8 fluid oz
300ml	10 fluid oz
500ml	16 fluid oz
600ml	20 fluid oz
1000ml (1 litre)	1¾ pints

LENGTH MEASURES

metric	imperial
3mm	⅛in
6mm	¼in
1cm	½in
2cm	¾in
2.5cm	1in
5cm	2in
6cm	2½in
8cm	3in
10cm	4in
13cm	5in
15cm	6in
18cm	7in
20cm	8in
22cm	9in
25cm	10in
28cm	11in
30cm	12in (1ft)

OVEN TEMPERATURES

The oven temperatures in this book are for conventional ovens; if you have a fan-forced oven, decrease the temperature by 10-20 degrees.

	°C (Celsius)	°F (Fahrenheit)
Very slow	120	250
Slow	150	300
Moderately slow	160	325
Moderate	180	350
Moderately hot	200	400
Hot	220	425
Very hot	240	475

Index

Anna Jones
The modern cook

I'm not a canapes person. They are fiddly, just one bite and there is only ever one vegetarian tray, which is always on the other side of the room ... If I am at a party, I want food that fills me up, is bright and enlivening, can be eaten with my hands and helps soak up some of the wine I plan to drink. A banh mi is my dream party food: crunch from some fresh veg, punch from the sriracha, and crisp-edged tofu. With this in one hand and a lemongrass margarita in the other, I'll be the last one on the dancefloor.

New Year's Eve banh mi

Prep	25 min
Cook	10 min
Serves	4

For the veg
100g radishes, sliced into thin matchsticks
½ green apple, sliced into thin matchsticks
¼ cucumber, sliced into thin matchsticks
1 medium carrot, sliced into thin matchsticks
1 tbsp rice-wine vinegar
1 tsp caster sugar
15g pickled ginger, plus 2 tbsp of the pickling juice

For the sriracha and lime mayonnaise
150g good mayonnaise
1 tbsp sriracha
Juice and zest of ½ lime

For the tofu
Sesame oil
250g firm tofu, sliced into 2cm strips
1 tsp runny honey or agave
3 tsp sesame seeds
Juice and zest of 1 lime
Flaky sea salt and black pepper
1 small bunch coriander, roughly chopped

To serve
1 large, soft and fluffy baguette
1 small bunch coriander, leaves picked
1 small bunch mint, leaves picked

You don't want a fancy sourdough baguette here: crusty baguettes are not a banh mi's friend. You want the lightest, softest, airiest baguette you can get your hands on. There are bakeries that make Vietnamese-style baguettes specifically for banh mi, so if you can get your hands on them, hats off to you. You can make the veg, mayo and tofu (keep the tofu warm in a low oven) ahead of time, and put the baguettes together as needed.

Mix all the veg ingredients in a bowl and set aside. In a small bowl, mix together the mayonnaise ingredients, then set aside.

Put two tablespoons of sesame oil in a large, nonstick frying pan, then fry the tofu for about five minutes, until crisp and golden on all sides.

Turn off the heat, then add the honey, followed by the sesame seeds, and toss to coat the tofu. Now add the lime juice and zest, with a good pinch of flaky sea salt and the coriander.

Warm the baguette in the oven, then cut in half lengthways, making sure that you don't slice all the way to the bottom. Spread the top and bottom with a layer of the sriracha mayo, followed by a layer of the pickled veg, then the tofu. Finish with a handful of coriander and mint leaves, then cut into quarters and serve while the tofu is still warm.

Thomasina Miers
The simple fix

This is a spectacular but incredibly easy feast for New Year. I try to save fish for high days and holidays: there's no better excuse than New Year's Eve for this quick-to-cook and suitably celebratory sea bass. I like to give it an Asian treatment, especially after all the rich flavours of Christmas. Try to find a local, Asian supermarket, because they often sell coriander with the root still attached (it has a sweet, heady taste). Then smash those Thai ingredients in a mortar and let the nuances of flavour captivate everyone at the table.

PHOTOGRAPH AND PROP STYLING: YUKI SUGIURA FOR THE GUARDIAN. FOOD STYLING: AYA NISHIMURA. FOOD ASSISTANT: SONALI SHAH. INSET: LOUISE HAGGER

Baked sea bass with lemongrass and nam jim

 GF DF

Prep	1 hr
Cook	25 min
Serves	4-6

1 large wild sea bass (about 800g)
Peanut or vegetable oil
Salt and pepper
2 lemongrass stalks
3 makrut lime leaves

For the nam jim
1 lemongrass stalks
2 bird's eye chillies, de-stalked and roughly chopped
2 fat garlic cloves, peeled
2 large bunches coriander (preferably with the roots still attached)
2 tsp palm or demerara sugar, to taste
2 tsp fish sauce
Juice of 4 limes
2 tbsp rice-wine vinegar

For the salad
½ Chinese leaf, shredded
4 handfuls beansprouts
2 handful coriander leaves
2 carrots, peeled and shredded
1 big handful mint leaves

To serve
Jasmine or coconut rice

The aromatic, garlicky and spicy dressing is utterly delicious with this simply baked fish – it's so good, I use it to dress the beansprout salad, too.

Heat the oven to 230C (210C fan)/gas 8. Lay the fish on an oiled piece of baking paper on a large baking tray. Rub the skin with more oil and season generously with salt. Bash and flatten the lemongrass stalks, combine with the lime leaves, and stuff into the cavity of the fish. Roast for 20-25 minutes.

Steam some jasmine or coconut rice; you can do this a few hours before your guests arrive, if you prefer. Keep somewhere warm, sealed with butter wrappers or buttery greaseproof paper and dressed with a drizzle of oil.

For the nam jim, peel the lemongrass stalk and slice the tender, inner core. Add to a large mortar (a small one won't work here, so use a food processor if you don't have a large one) with the chilli, garlic, coriander and a large pinch of salt, and smash to a rough paste. Add the palm sugar, work in for another 30 seconds, then add the fish sauce. This can be done an hour or two in advance. When you are ready to eat, add the lime juice, taste and adjust for sweetness, heat, salt and sourness.

Transfer half the nam jim to a large salad bowl with the rice-wine vinegar. Add the salad ingredients and some seasoning, and combine with your hands until everything is nicely coated. Serve with the fish, rice and the rest of the nam jim.

The Guardian aims to publish recipes for fish rated as sustainable by the Marine Conservation Society's Good Fish Guide.

Palak tofu

Prep	30 min
Cook	50 min
Serves	4 as a main

Salt and black pepper
2 x 280g blocks extra-firm tofu (I use an organic one), patted dry and cut into 2cm cubes
500g baby spinach
20g coriander leaves, roughly chopped
75ml olive oil
1 large onion, peeled and finely chopped (200g net weight)
6 garlic cloves, peeled and finely chopped
40g fresh ginger, peeled and finely chopped
1 large green chilli, finely chopped, seeds and all
2 plum tomatoes, finely chopped
1 tbsp each coriander and cumin seeds, roughly crushed in a mortar
¼ tsp ground turmeric
1 tbsp kasoori methi (dried fenugreek leaves)
½ tsp Aleppo chilli

This vegan take on palak paneer uses tofu soaked in a salt brine, but you can also use other vegan alternatives such as butterbeans or roast cauliflower. Kasoori methi are dried fenugreek leaves and can be found on the world food aisle of most supermarkets, and in specialist Indian and Middle Eastern stores. Serve this with plain rice or naan.

In a large, heatproof bowl, dissolve a tablespoon of salt in 700ml boiling hot water. Add the tofu, leave to soak for 20 minutes (this helps season it all the way through), then drain and set aside.

Meanwhile, bring a large pot of water to a boil. Add the spinach, press it down with a spoon to submerge and blanch for about 45 seconds, until just wilted. Drain into a sieve, then run under the cold tap until it's no longer warm to the touch. Leave the spinach to drain for no more than 10 minutes, then, without squeezing out any of the excess water, put it in a blender with the coriander leaves and blitz to a smooth paste – you may have to scrape down the sides of the blender a few times as you go. Spoon the mix into a bowl and set aside, then put 300ml water in the blender and swirl it around to pick up any remaining spinach.

Put three tablespoons of oil in a large saute pan on a medium-high heat. Once hot, fry the onion for about seven minutes, stirring occasionally, until soft and golden. Add the garlic, ginger and chilli, and fry, stirring, for four minutes more, until fragrant and browned. Set aside about a third of this mixture, then stir in the tomatoes, two-thirds each of the cumin and coriander, all the turmeric, kasoori methi and quarter-teaspoon of salt into the pan. Cook for four minutes, stirring often, until the tomatoes have completely broken down, then add the pureed spinach, the spinachy water from the blender, the tofu, a teaspoon of salt and a good grind of pepper, and bring to a gentle simmer. Cook for seven minutes, stirring occasionally, until the tofu has warmed through and the sauce has come together.

Meanwhile, lightly toast the remaining cumin and coriander seeds, then add to the bowl with the reserved onion mixture and stir in the remaining two tablespoons of oil.

Transfer the curry to a shallow platter, spoon the onion mixture all over the top, sprinkle with the Aleppo chilli and serve.

Yotam Ottolenghi

There's a fuzzy period between Christmas and New Year when no one quite remembers what the date or plan is. Festive gatherings continue, all fuelled by food, drink and good cheer. That's the theory, anyway. A spread of shareable dishes is a very good place to start in terms of bringing everyone together in putting the year to bed around the table. Break and share some bread, and crack a few eggs to signal new life – it's a new year, and a new decade! Happy new year, all. Eat and be well.

PHOTOGRAPHS: LOUISE HAGGER FOR THE GUARDIAN. FOOD STYLING: EMILY KYDD. PROP STYLING: LOUIE WALLER. FOOD ASSISTANT: KATY GILHOOLY & CAROLE HECTOR. PHOTO ASSISTANT: SAM REEVES

V Vegetarian

VG Vegan

GF Gluten free

DF Dairy free

Yoghurt rice with chana dal and curry leaf oil

 V **GF**

Prep	20 min
Cook	1 hr 5 min
Serves	4

100g chana dal, soaked in plenty of cold water for at least two hours (and ideally overnight)
200g basmati rice, washed until the water runs clear, then drained
135ml olive oil
Salt and black pepper
1 large egg yolk
200g Greek-style yoghurt
1 large onion, peeled and finely chopped
6 garlic cloves, peeled and crushed
30g fresh ginger, peeled and finely grated
2 green chillies, 1 finely chopped, the other thinly sliced (remove the pith and seeds if you prefer less heat)
1 tsp garam masala
3 dried red chillies (the mild, finger-length type)
20 curry leaves (ie, from about 2 stems)
1 tsp black mustard seeds
¼ tsp ground turmeric

There's something super-comforting about the combination of rice and yoghurt. This take on Indian curd rice is quite spicy, so reduce (or ditch) the chilli if you want a more kid-friendly meal. You can make the rice in advance, but thin it out with a little water when reheating. Serve this as a light meal with some gently cooked greens.

Drain the soaked chana dal, then put in a small saucepan with enough cold water to cover by about 3cm. Bring to a boil on a medium-high heat, then simmer for 15-30 minutes, until the dal is cooked but still holds its shape. (Timings can vary greatly depending on soaking time, so be sure to test it at the 15-minute mark, and allow more time as needed.) Drain into a sieve, then run under the cold tap to stop the dal cooking further.

Fill a large saucepan with 1.3 litres water, bring to a boil on a medium-high heat, then keep hot on a low heat.

Put the rice, two tablespoons of oil, 200ml of the hot water and one and three-quarter teaspoons of salt into a large saute pan on a medium-high heat. Bring to a simmer, stirring often, until most of the water has been absorbed, then repeat, adding 200ml hot water at a time and stirring often, until you have used up 1.2 litres of the water and the rice resembles a loose, creamy porridge (it will be overcooked) – this will take about 20 minutes. Lightly crush the rice grains with the back of a spoon – you don't want to mash them completely – then turn down the heat to medium-low.

In a bowl, whisk the egg yolk, yoghurt and 50ml of the hot water until smooth, then stir the yoghurt mix into the rice and cook, stirring often, for about seven minutes, until the mixture has thickened slightly, but is still a loose porridge.

While the rice is cooking, make the topping. Put three tablespoons of oil in a large frying pan on a medium-high heat. Add the onion and cook, stirring occasionally, until softened and browned – about eight minutes. Add the garlic, ginger and chopped green chilli, and cook for four minutes more, until fragrant. Stir through the chana dal, garam masala, 60ml water, three-quarters of a teaspoon of salt and a good grind of pepper, and cook, stirring occasionally, until the chana dal starts to brown in places – about 10 minutes. Transfer to a bowl and cover to keep warm.

Wipe out the pan and return it to a medium-high heat. Add the remaining four tablespoons of oil and the dried and sliced chillies, and cook for three minutes, until starting to soften but not colour. Add the curry leaves, cook for another minute, until translucent, then stir in the mustard seeds and turmeric, and remove from the heat.

To serve, divide the curd rice between four shallow bowls and top with the chana dal mixture. Drizzle all over with the curry leaf oil and its solids, and serve warm. →